W9-CXT-274

THINKERS
AND THEORIES
IN ETHICS

THE BRITANNICA GUIDE TO ETHICS

THINKERS
AND THEORIES
IN ETHICS

EDITED BY BRIAN DUIGNAN, SENIOR EDITOR, PHILOSOPHY AND RELIGION

Britannica
Educational Publishing

IN ASSOCIATION WITH

ROSEN
EDUCATIONAL SERVICES

Published in 2011 by Britannica Educational Publishing
(a trademark of Encyclopædia Britannica, Inc.)
in association with Rosen Educational Services, LLC
29 East 21st Street, New York, NY 10010.

Distributed exclusively by Rosen Educational Services.
For a listing of additional Britannica Educational Publishing titles, call toll free (800) 237-9932.

First Edition

Britannica Educational Publishing
Michael I. Levy: Executive Editor
J.E. Luebering: Senior Manager
Marilyn L. Barton: Senior Coordinator, Production Control
Steven Bosco: Director, Editorial Technologies
Lisa S. Braucher: Senior Producer and Data Editor
Yvette Charboneau: Senior Copy Editor
Kathy Nakamura: Manager, Media Acquisition
Brian Duignan: Senior Editor, Philosophy and Religion

Rosen Educational Services
Heather M. Moore Niver: Editor
Nelson Sá: Art Director
Cindy Reiman: Photography Manager
Matthew Cauli: Designer, Cover Design
Introduction by Brian Duignan

Library of Congress Cataloging-in-Publication Data

Thinkers and theories in ethics / edited by Brian Duignan in association with Britannica Educational Publishing, Rosen Education Services.—1st ed.
  p. cm.—(The Britannica guide to ethics)
"In association with Britannica Educational Publishing, Rosen Educational Services."
Includes bibliographical references and index.
ISBN 978-1-61530-311-3 (library binding)
1. Ethics. I. Duignan, Brian.
BJ71.T45 2011
170—dc22

2010018911

Manufactured in the United States of America

On the cover: Shutterstock.com

CONTENTS

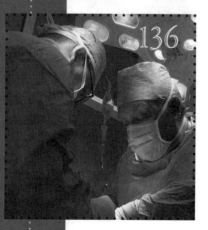

INTRODUCTION

Ethics is the philosophical study of morality. For most of its history, it has been occupied with two main tasks: to discover what moral qualities such as right and wrong, good and bad consist of—what it means to say that an action is right, that a thing or event is bad, and so on—and to investigate certain broader questions regarding the nature and scope of morality and moral judgments. Such general questions have included, for example, whether moral judgments are statements of fact or merely expressions of feeling or attitude; how moral facts, if they exist, can be known; whether a single morality can be valid for all people in all societies at all times; how to reconcile the practice of moral praise and blame with the apparent fact that every human action is causally determined; and whether there is a compelling reason to behave morally at all times, even in situations in which one has something to gain—and nothing to lose— by behaving immorally. The first task is the province of what is called normative ethics, the philosophical study of moral norms or standards, the second that of theoretical ethics, or "metaethics." A third and more recent field, consisting of the application of normative ethical theories to practical problems, is appropriately known as applied ethics.

Among normative-ethical theories, the most influential belong to one of four broad types: consequentialist, deontological, contractual, and eudaemonistic. Consequentialist theories have in common the view that the rightness or wrongness of an action depends solely on its consequences. Typically, such theories claim that an action is right if it

Ethics pertains to animals as well as humans, particularly given the violent abuse of animals in modern society. Dimitri Vervitsiotis/Photographer's Choice/Getty Images

produces a maximum amount of "good" or a minimum amount of "bad," and wrong if it does otherwise. Other varieties of consequentialism recognize gradations of rightness and wrongness, so that one action may be morally better (or worse) than another to the extent that it produces more (or less) good, or less (or more) bad. Some consequentialists, such as Jeremy Bentham (1748–1832) and John Stuart Mill (1806–73), have identified the good with pleasure or happiness, narrowly or broadly construed, and the bad with pain or unhappiness. Others have conceived of the good more generally as the satisfaction of desires and the bad as the frustration of desires — the right action then being the one that creates the most desire satisfaction or the least desire frustration. Still other consequentialists — notably G.E. Moore (1873–1958) — have recognized a plurality of goods to be maximized or increased, including, in addition to pleasure and happiness, beauty, knowledge, freedom, and friendship.

Deontological ethical theories hold that the rightness or wrongness of an action is determined, primarily or exclusively, by whether it is consistent with a given moral rule or principle. Consequences are of secondary importance or of no importance at all. The rule in question may apply primarily to the person who performs the action (the agent), such as "do not lie," or to the person whom the action affects (the patient), such as "no person should be used for another's benefit without his or her consent." Rules of the former sort are usually understood to express a duty or obligation of the agent, and rules of the latter sort to express a right of the patient (in this case a right to a certain measure of autonomy or a right not to be used against one's will). The foremost representative of deontological ethics remains Immanuel Kant (1724–1804).

Some philosophers treat contractualist theories as a subspecies of deontology, insofar as such theories tend to emphasize rules or principles rather than consequences. According to some versions of contractualism—for example, that of Thomas Hobbes (1588–1679)—an action is right if it is consistent with a rule that each person would agree to observe on the condition that everyone else does the same. Other versions—for example, that of John Rawls (1921–2002)—hold that the rule must be one that each person would accept or prefer in an ideal set of decision-making circumstances—one in which the person is, among other things, rational, informed of the relevant facts, clear-headed, and not mentally or emotionally disturbed.

Finally, eudaemonism, the most ancient type of normative ethical theory, is distinct from the other types insofar as it is concerned with understanding the "good life," in the broadest sense of that term, and with identifying what is necessary for and constitutive of that life, especially including good traits of character, or virtues. Epitomized in the ethics of Plato (c. 428–348 BCE) and Aristotle (384–322 BCE), eudaemonism was the dominant form of nonreligious ethical theory until the 17th century, when it was eclipsed by contractualism and later by consequentialism. Since its revival in the mid-20th century, it has been better known as "virtue theory," a name that justly reflects the modern version's greater emphasis on virtue and character over the good life per se.

It is significant that since the end of the ancient period in the history of Western philosophy (c. 500 CE) there has never been a time during which one of these types of theory was dominant. This is partly because each type is general enough to admit numerous variations through which potential objections may be overcome. Perhaps more importantly, it is also because each type seems able to capture moral intuitions that the others have trouble accounting for; each reflects important aspects of moral thinking and experience that the others seem to neglect.

This fact is especially evident in the contrast between consequentialism and deontology. In ordinary moral decision-making, sometimes the consequences of an action seem the most important factor to weigh, and sometimes one's duties or another's rights seem most important. This is true even in cases in which the two considerations coincide — that is, they recommend the same course of action. When the considerations do conflict, however, it may be unclear which should take precedence. In truth, most people have both consequentialist and deontological moral intuitions. The greatest challenge to proponents of both types of theory, therefore, is to make revisions or elaborations that are significant enough to account for problematic moral intuitions but not so significant that they rob the theory of its basic character as consequentialist or deontological.

Much of the modern history of each type of theory can be understood as a series of refinements made in response to objections from the other types. A conventional criticism of consequentialism, for example, is that it permits unjustly inflicting a great deal of bad upon one person (or a few people) in cases when doing so would produce a maximum (or a greater) amount of good for everyone else. A standard type of example is that of a person in a small town who is falsely accused of murder. A judge with the power to pronounce innocence or guilt knows that the defendant is innocent but cannot convince the townspeople, who have gathered in a mob to demand an execution. Surely the judge should not declare the defendant guilty just to satisfy the mob, but consequentialism seems to recommend that he should. In contrast, deontology can account for this intuition by positing a rule that the judge's action would violate, such as "do not facilitate the killing of innocent people."

Many consequentialists have responded to this objection by claiming that it does not take into account the full range of consequences of the judge's action, among which would be that, from then on, many people in the town would live in constant fear of being falsely accused. Such a response is weak, however, because it is always possible to imagine circumstances in which whatever the good is created for the mob far outweighs the bad created for the fearful townspeople.

Other consequentialists have held that such cases show the need for an innovation in their theory. They have proposed that what makes an action right or wrong is whether it accords with a moral rule, and what justifies a moral rule is the fact that its general adoption would produce a greater amount of good than would the general adoption of some other rule. Presumably, this criterion would justify a rule such as "do not facilitate the killing of innocent people," so the judge should not declare the defendant guilty.

One problem with this refinement, however, is that it is not clear that there can be a principled distinction between consequentialism as applied to rules and consequentialism as applied to actions. As the example of the judge and the mob illustrates, for almost any rule the consequentialist may propose, it is possible to imagine a case in which following it would have worse consequences than not following it. If this were true, a rule that made an exception for just that case would have better consequences, if it were generally adopted, than a rule that made no exceptions. But if a rule that made one exception would have better consequences than a rule that made none, a rule that made all possible exceptions would have the best consequences of all. The problem is that following such a super-qualified rule would be no different from judging each action on the basis its own consequences. "Rule" consequentialism thus collapses into "act" consequentialism, and the original objection retains its force.

Examples of the judge-and-mob type seem to favour a deontological approach. However, deontological theories also face serious difficulties. Suppose, for example, that it were possible to save the lives of several million people by killing only one innocent person: the all-consuming love interest of a murderous dictator, who is likely to give up his plans of world domination if the object of his affections is removed. A deontological theory that contains the rule "do not facilitate the killing of innocent people" (or, more directly, "do not kill the innocent") would thus entail that in some cases people have a duty to bring about suffering on a catastrophic scale. Many people find this kind of commitment strongly counterintuitive.

One possible deontological response relies on distinguishing between the moral status of the act and the moral status of the agent. Although the act of killing the dictator's love interest is wrong, the agent is praiseworthy because of the good consequences the killing brings about. Some critics of deontology, however, have argued that this response evades the issue.

A closely related problem for deontology is that, in real life, moral rules often conflict with each other. Another standard example is that of a person in a Nazi-occupied country who is hiding Jews in his attic. He is arrested, and at one point his interrogator asks him whether he is hiding Jews. Here the rule "do not facilitate the killing of innocent people" conflicts with the rule "do not lie." How is one to know which rule takes precedence? The deontologist may choose to follow the rule that results in the best consequences, but then his or her theory would begin to sound like rule-consequentialism. The act-consequentialist, in contrast, can easily account for the intuition that the person being interrogated should lie.

How would contractualist and eudaemonistic theories handle such cases? Consider the variety of contractualism according to which the rule that applies is the one that each person would accept if he or she were perfectly rational, informed of the relevant facts, and so on. Presumably, people in such circumstances would accept a rule such as "do not lie." But they would also accept "do not facilitate the killing of innocent people." If they accept both, how are cases of conflict to be resolved? Perhaps such people would accept a "meta-rule" that states: a rule takes precedence if following it would have the best consequences. But then the contractualist, like the mainstream deontologist, seems to be heading down the path toward rule-consequentialism.

Because eudaemonistic theories are primarily concerned with human virtue and vice, they can be applied only indirectly to actions. Yet it has been proposed by some eudaemonists that right actions are those that express or cultivate or strengthen virtues such as honesty, integrity, and beneficence (among many others). In the cases at hand, however, it is at best unclear which action would meet this standard. Indeed, it seems that both actions would do so, though the virtues affected are different.

This brief survey hardly does justice to the breadth and sophistication of these theories or to the complexity of the moral problems they address. This book will explore these problems in detail while introducing the reader to the most influential ethical philosophers in history.

CHAPTER 1

NORMATIVE ETHICS: EUDAEMONISM AND CONSEQUENTIALISM

N ormative ethics is the branch of ethics (also called moral philosophy) that is concerned with the moral evaluation of human actions, institutions, and ways of life. The central task of normative ethics is to determine how basic moral standards, or norms, are justified and what basic norms there may be. Two important approaches to this task, eudaemonism and consequentialism, are discussed in this chapter. Other approaches, namely contractualism, deontology, feminism, and egoism, are treated in Chapter 2.

EUDAEMONISM

Eudaemonism derives its name from the ancient Greek word *eudaimonia,* which literally means "the state of having a good indwelling spirit." The usual English rendering of this term, "happiness," is an inadequate translation, however, because it incorrectly suggests that *eudaimonia* is simply a mood or a state of mind. It is instead the condition of living a good life, sometimes called a life of "human flourishing." According to eudaemonistic theories, right or virtuous action is that which enables, brings about, or is constitutive of happiness in this sense. The best known forms of eudaemonism are those of Plato (*c.* 428–*c.* 348 BCE), Aristotle (384–322 BCE), and the Stoics.

THE ETHICS OF PLATO

In ancient Greek philosophy the notion of *arete* — "virtue" or "excellence" — applies to anything that has a characteristic use, function, or activity: the excellence of that thing is whatever disposition enables it (and things of the same kind) to perform well. The excellence of a racehorse is whatever enables it to run well; the excellence of a knife is whatever enables it to cut well; and the excellence of an eye is whatever enables it to see well. Human virtue, accordingly, is whatever enables human beings to live the best possible human life, in other words, to be happy.

Ancient Greek culture recognized a conventional set of virtues, which included courage, justice, piety, modesty or temperance, and wisdom. Plato and his teacher, Socrates (*c.* 470–399 BCE), undertook to discover what these virtues really amount to. A truly satisfactory account of any virtue would identify what it is, show how possessing it enables one to live well, and indicate how it is best acquired.

Because Socrates wrote nothing, almost all of what is known about his philosophy is derived from the portrayal of him in several of Plato's dialogues, especially the early (or "Socratic") dialogues. In these works, a character called "Socrates" is represented in conversation with various prominent figures, often in a search for a definition of a particular virtue (e.g., courage, justice, piety, temperance, or wisdom). According to Socrates, all that is needed to live a happy life is to be perfectly virtuous, and all that is needed to possess a particular virtue is to know what it is. But it is exceedingly difficult to obtain this kind of knowledge, as the failures of his interlocutors

Justice is just one of a group of conventional virtues recognized by ancient Greek culture. Library of Congress Prints and Photographs Division

dramatically demonstrate. (Indeed, the historical Socrates himself professed not to know what the virtues are.) This is partly because the definitions Socrates searches for are not the sort of thing one would find in a dictionary. Rather, they are general accounts of the "real nature" of the thing in question. (The real definition of *water*, for example, is H_2O, though this fact was unknown in most historical eras.) In the encounters Plato portrays, the interlocutors typically offer an example of the virtue they are asked to define (not the right kind of answer) or give a general account (the right kind of answer) that is inconsistent with their intuitions on related matters.

Because the virtues, according to Socrates, are a kind of knowledge, anyone who knows what a particular virtue is will necessarily act in accordance with it. If one knows, for example, what courage or piety is, one will act courageously or piously, and similarly for all the other virtues. It follows that anyone who fails to act virtuously does so because he incorrectly identifies virtue (or a particular virtue) with something it is not. Socrates' view also implies that weakness of will, what the Greeks called *akrasia*—knowingly acting in a way one believes to be wrong—is impossible. Aristotle, the greatest student of Plato, rejected this view as plainly at odds with the facts.

TREATMENT OF VIRTUE IN THE EARLY DIALOGUES

The early dialogues of Plato are generally short and entertaining and fairly accessible, even to readers with no background in philosophy. Indeed, they were probably intended by Plato to draw such readers into the subject.

In 399 BCE Socrates was brought to trial on charges of impiety and corrupting the young. He was convicted and sentenced to death by poison. The *Apology* represents the speech that Socrates gave in his defense at his trial, and it gives an interpretation of Socrates' career: he has been a "gadfly," trying to awaken the noble horse of Athens to an awareness of virtue, and he is wisest in the sense that he is aware that he knows nothing.

Each of the other early dialogues represents a particular Socratic encounter. Thus in the *Charmides*, Socrates discusses temperance and self-knowledge with Critias and Charmides. The dialogue moves from an account in terms of behaviour ("temperance is a kind of quietness") to an attempt to specify the underlying state that accounts for it; the latter effort breaks down in puzzles over the reflexive application of knowledge.

The *Crito* shows Socrates in prison, discussing why he chooses not to escape before the death sentence is carried out. The dialogue considers the source and nature of political obligation. The *Euthyphro* asks, "What is piety?" Euthyphro fails to maintain the successive positions that piety is "what the gods love," "what the gods all love," or some sort of service to the gods. Socrates and Euthyphro agree that what they seek is a single form, present in all things that are pious, that makes them so. Socrates suggests that if Euthyphro could specify what part of justice piety is, he would have an account.

The more elaborate *Gorgias* considers, while its namesake is at Athens, whether orators command a genuine art or merely have a knack of flattery. Socrates holds that the arts of the legislator and the judge address the health of the soul, which orators counterfeit by taking the pleasant instead of the good as their standard. Discussion of whether one should envy the man who can bring about any result he likes leads to a Socratic paradox: it is better to suffer wrong than to do it. Callicles praises the man of natural ability who ignores conventional justice. True justice, according to Callicles, is this person's triumph. In the *Hippias Minor*, discussion of the epic poet Homer by a visiting Sophist (a professional—and usually cynical—teacher of rhetoric and logic) leads to an examination by Socrates, which the Sophist fails, on such questions as whether a just person who does wrong on purpose is better than other wrongdoers.

The interlocutors in the *Laches* are generals. Here the observation that the sons of great men often do not turn out well leads to an examination of what courage is. The trend again is from an account in terms of behaviour ("standing fast in battle") to an attempt to specify the inner state that underlies it ("knowledge of the grounds of hope and fear"), but none of the participants displays adequate understanding of these suggestions. The *Lysis* is an examination of the nature of friendship. The work introduces the notion of a primary object of love, for whose sake one loves other things.

The *Meno* takes up the familiar question of whether virtue can be taught, and, if so, why eminent men have not been able to bring up their sons to be virtuous. Concerned with method, the dialogue develops Meno's problem: How is it possible to search either for what one knows (for one already knows it) or for what one does not know (and so could not look for)? This is answered by the recollection theory of learning. What is called learning is really prompted recollection. One possesses all theoretical knowledge latently at birth, as demonstrated by the slave boy's ability to solve geometry problems when properly prompted. The dialogue is also famous as an early discussion of the distinction between knowledge and true belief.

The *Protagoras*, another discussion with a visiting Sophist, concerns whether virtue can be taught and whether the different virtues are really one. The dialogue contains yet another discussion of the phenomenon that the sons of the great are often undistinguished. Most famously, this dialogue develops the characteristic

Socratic suggestion that virtue is identical with wisdom and discusses the Socratic position that *akrasia* is impossible.

THE *REPUBLIC*

The middle dialogues of Plato have similar agendas. Although they are primarily concerned with ethical and other human issues, they also proclaim the importance of metaphysical inquiry and sketch Plato's doctrine of forms, which Socrates certainly did not hold. According to this doctrine, corresponding to every property or feature that a particular thing may have, there is an unchanging and eternal reality, called a form, in which the thing "participates." Thus, having a property is a matter of participating in the corresponding form. For example, Achilles is beautiful by virtue of the fact that he participates in the form of Beauty, and the racehorse War Emblem is black by virtue of his participating in the form of Blackness. Likewise, being courageous, just, or pious or possessing any of the other human virtues consists of participating in the form of Courage, Justice, or Piety, and so on. Such forms, according to Plato, are what Socrates and his interlocutors were searching for in their struggle to discover the real definitions of the virtues. However, Plato does not fully specify how the forms are to be understood until the later dialogues, particularly the *Parmenides*.

In one of the greatest dialogues of the middle period, the *Republic*, Plato develops a view of happiness and virtue that departs from that of Socrates. According to Plato, there are three parts of the soul—reason, spirit, and appetite—each of which has its own natural object of desire. Thus, reason desires truth and the good of the individual as a whole, spirit desires the honour and esteem

7

obtained through competition, and appetite desires sensually appealing things such as food, drink, and sex. The happy individual, for Plato, is the one in whom the three parts of the soul act in harmony, each desiring what it is appropriate for it to desire and none becoming so dominant that it frustrates the desires of the other two.

Although the dialogue starts from the question "Why should I be just?," Socrates proposes that this inquiry can be advanced by examining justice "writ large" in an ideal city. Thus, the political discussion is undertaken to aid the ethical one. One early hint of the existence of the three parts of the soul in the individual is the existence of three classes in the well-functioning state: rulers, guardians, and producers. The wise state is the one in which the rulers understand the good; the courageous state is that in which the guardians can retain in the heat of battle the judgments handed down by the rulers about what is to be feared; the temperate state is that in which all citizens agree about who is to rule; and the just state is that in which each of the three classes does its own work properly. Thus, for the city to be fully virtuous, each citizen must contribute appropriately.

Justice as conceived in the *Republic* is so comprehensive that a person who possessed it would also possess all the other virtues, thereby achieving happiness, or "the health of that whereby we live [the soul]." Yet, lest it be thought that habituation and correct instruction in human affairs alone can lead to this condition, one must keep in view that the *Republic* also develops the famous doctrine according to which reason cannot properly understand the human good or anything else without grasping the Good itself. Thus the original inquiry, whose starting point was a motivation each individual is presumed to have (to learn how to live well), leads to a highly ambitious educational program. Starting with exposure only to salutary stories, poetry,

According to Plato's doctrine of forms, Achilles is beautiful by virtue of the fact that he takes part in the form of Beauty. The Bridgeman Art Library/ Getty Images

and music from childhood and continuing with supervised habituation to good action and years of training in a series of mathematical disciplines, this program—and so virtue—would be complete only in the person who was able to grasp the first principle, the Good, and to proceed on that basis to secure accounts of the other realities.

THE ETHICS OF ARISTOTLE

The surviving works of Aristotle include three treatises on moral philosophy: the *Nicomachean Ethics* in 10 books, the *Eudemian Ethics* in 7 books, and the *Magna moralia* (Latin: "Great Ethics"). The *Nicomachean Ethics* is generally regarded as the most important of the three; it consists of a series of short treatises, possibly brought together by Aristotle's son Nicomachus. It is also probable that Aristotle used the *Eudemian Ethics* for a course on ethics that he taught at the school he founded, the Lyceum, during his mature period. The *Magna moralia* probably consists of notes taken by an unknown student of such a course.

HAPPINESS

Aristotle's approach to ethics is teleological. If life is to be worth living, he argues, it must surely be for the sake of something that is an end in itself (i.e., desirable for its own sake). Therefore, the highest human good, which Aristotle calls happiness, must be desirable for its own sake, and all other goods must be desirable for the sake of it. One popular conception of the highest human good is pleasure—the pleasures of food, drink, and sex, combined with aesthetic and intellectual pleasures. Other people prefer a life of virtuous action in the political sphere. A third possible candidate for the highest human good is scientific or philosophical contemplation. Aristotle thus

Soul

The soul is the purported immaterial aspect or essence of a human being, that which confers individuality and humanity. It is often identified with the mind or the self.

Many cultures have recognized some incorporeal principle corresponding to the soul, and many have attributed souls to all living things. Both the ancient Egyptians and the ancient Chinese conceived of a dual soul. The Egyptian *ka* (breath) survived death but remained near the body, while the spiritual *ba* proceeded to the region of the dead. The Chinese distinguished between a lower, sensitive soul, which disappears with death, and a rational principle, the *hun,* which survives the grave and is the object of ancestor worship. The ancient Hebrews apparently had a concept of the soul but did not separate it from the body, although later Jewish writers developed the idea of the soul further.

Ancient Greek concepts of the soul varied considerably. For the Platonists, the soul was an immaterial and incorporeal substance. Aristotle's conception of the soul was obscure, though he did state that it was a form inseparable from the body. Socrates and Plato accepted the immortality of the soul, while Aristotle considered only part of the soul, the *noûs,* or intellect, to have that quality. The early Christian philosophers adopted the Greek concept of the soul's immortality and thought of the soul as being created by God and infused into the body at conception.

Among early-modern philosophers, René Descartes believed that human beings were a union of the body and the soul, each a distinct substance acting on the other, while Benedict de Spinoza held that body and soul are but two aspects of a single reality.

In Hinduism the *atman* ("breath," or "soul") is the universal, eternal self, of which each individual soul (*jiva* or *jiva-atman*) partakes. The *jiva-atman* is also eternal but is imprisoned in an earthly body at birth. At death the *jiva-atman* passes into a new existence determined by karma, or the cumulative consequences of actions. Buddhism asserts that any sense of having an individual eternal soul or of partaking in a persistent universal self is illusory. The Muslim concept, like the Christian, holds that the soul comes into existence at the same time as the body. Thereafter, it has a life of its own, its union with the body being a temporary condition.

reduces the answers to the question "What is the good human life?" to a short list of three: the philosophical life, the political life, and the voluptuary life. This triad provides the key to his ethical inquiry.

According to Aristotle, human beings must have a function, because particular types of humans (e.g., sculptors) do, as do the parts and organs of individual human beings. Because this function must be unique to humans, it cannot consist of growth and nourishment, for this is shared by plants, or the life of the senses, for this is shared by animals. It must therefore involve the peculiarly human faculty of reason. The highest human good is the same as good human functioning, and good human functioning is the same as the good exercise of the faculty of reason—that is to say, the activity of rational soul in accordance with virtue. There are two kinds of virtue: moral and intellectual. Moral virtues are exemplified by courage, temperance, and liberality; the key intellectual virtues are wisdom, which governs ethical behaviour, and understanding, which is expressed in scientific endeavour and contemplation.

VIRTUE

People's virtues are a subset of their good qualities. They are not innate, like eyesight, but are acquired by practice and lost by disuse. They are abiding states, and they thus differ from momentary passions such as anger and pity. Virtues are states of character that find expression both in purpose and in action. Moral virtue is expressed in good purpose—that is to say, in prescriptions for action in accordance with a good plan of life. It is expressed also in actions that avoid both excess and defect. A temperate person, for example, will avoid eating or drinking too much, but he will also avoid eating or drinking too little. Virtue chooses the mean, or middle ground, between excess and defect. Besides purpose and action, virtue is also concerned with feeling. One may, for example, be excessively concerned with sex or insufficiently interested in it; the temperate person will take the appropriate degree of interest and be neither lustful nor frigid.

While all the moral virtues are means of action and passion, it is not the case that every kind of action and passion is capable of a virtuous mean. There are some actions of which there is no right amount, because any amount of them is too much. Aristotle gives murder and adultery as examples. The virtues, besides being concerned with means of action and passion, are themselves means in the sense that they occupy a middle ground between two contrary vices. Thus, the virtue of courage is flanked on one side by foolhardiness and on the other by cowardice.

Aristotle's account of virtue as a mean is no truism. It is a distinctive ethical theory that contrasts with other influential systems of various kinds. Although it contrasts with deontological systems that give a central role to the concept of a moral rule or law, it also differs from moral systems such as utilitarianism that judge the rightness and wrongness of actions in terms of their consequences. Unlike the utilitarian, Aristotle believes that there are some kinds of action that are morally wrong in principle.

The mean that is the mark of moral virtue is determined by the intellectual virtue of wisdom. Wisdom is characteristically expressed in the formulation of prescriptions for action—"practical syllogisms," as Aristotle calls them. A practical syllogism consists of a general recipe for a good life, followed by an accurate description of the agent's actual circumstances and concluding with a decision about the appropriate action to be carried out.

Wisdom, the intellectual virtue that is proper to practical reason, is inseparably linked with the moral virtues of the affective part of the soul. Only if an agent possesses moral virtue will he endorse an appropriate recipe for a good life. Only if he is gifted with intelligence will he make an accurate assessment of the circumstances in which his decision is to be made. It is impossible, Aristotle says, to be really good without wisdom or to be really wise without moral virtue. Only when correct reasoning and right desire come together does truly virtuous action result.

ACTION AND CONTEMPLATION

The pleasures that are the domain of temperance, intemperance, and incontinence are the familiar bodily pleasures of food, drink, and sex. In treating of pleasure, however, Aristotle explores a much wider field. There are two classes of aesthetic pleasures: the pleasures of the inferior senses of touch and taste, and the pleasures of the superior senses of sight, hearing, and smell. Finally, at the top of the scale, there are the pleasures of the mind.

Plato had posed the question of whether the best life consists in the pursuit of pleasure or the exercise of the intellectual virtues. Aristotle's answer is that, properly understood, the two are not in competition with each other. The exercise of the highest form of virtue is the very same thing as the truest form of pleasure; each is identical with the other and with happiness. The highest virtues are the intellectual ones, and among them Aristotle distinguished between wisdom and understanding. To the question of whether happiness is to be identified with the pleasure of wisdom or with the pleasure of understanding, Aristotle gives different answers in his main ethical treatises. In the *Nicomachean Ethics* perfect happiness, though it presupposes the moral virtues, is constituted solely by the activity of philosophical contemplation, whereas in the *Eudemian Ethics* it consists in the harmonious exercise of all the virtues, intellectual and moral.

The Eudemian ideal of happiness, given the role it assigns to contemplation, to the moral virtues, and to pleasure, can claim to combine the features of the traditional three lives—the life of the philosopher, the life of the politician, and the life of the pleasure seeker. The happy person will value contemplation above all, but part of his happy life will consist in the exercise of moral virtues in the political sphere and the enjoyment in moderation of the natural human pleasures of body as well as of soul. But even in the *Eudemian Ethics* it is "the service and contemplation of God" that sets the standard for the appropriate exercise of the moral virtues, and in the *Nicomachean Ethics* this contemplation is described as a superhuman activity of a divine part of human nature. Aristotle's final word on ethics is that, despite being mortal, human beings must strive to make themselves immortal as far as they can.

STOICISM

Stoicism was a school of thought that flourished in Greek and Roman antiquity from about the 3rd century BCE. It was one of the loftiest and most sublime philosophies in the record of Western civilization. For the Stoics, the goal of human beings, the greatest good to which they can aspire, consists of living according to nature, in agreement with the world design.

THE NATURE OF STOICISM

For the early Stoic philosopher, as for all the post-Aristotelian schools, knowledge and its pursuit are no longer held to be ends in themselves. The Hellenistic Age was a time of transition, and the Stoic philosopher was perhaps its most influential representative. A new culture was in the making. The heritage of an earlier period, with Athens as its intellectual leader, was to continue, but to undergo many changes. If, as with Socrates, to know is to know oneself, rationality as the sole means by which something outside of the self might be achieved may be said to be the hallmark of Stoic belief. As a Hellenistic philosophy, Stoicism presented an *ars vitae,* a way of accommodation for people to whom the human condition no longer appeared as the mirror of a universal, calm, and ordered existence. Reason alone could reveal the constancy of cosmic order and the originative source of unyielding value; thus, reason became the true model for human existence. For the Stoic, virtue is an inherent feature of the world, no less inexorable in relation to humanity than are the laws of nature.

For the Stoics, the world is composed of material things, with some few exceptions, and the irreducible element in all things is right reason, which pervades the world as divine fire. Things, such as material, or corporeal, bodies, are governed by this reason or fate, in which virtue is inherent. The world in its awesome entirety is so ruled as to exhibit a grandeur of orderly arrangement that can only serve as a standard for humankind in the regulation and ordering of life.

Stoic moral theory is also based on the view that the world, as one great city, is a unity. Human beings, as world citizens, have an obligation and loyalty to all things in that city. They must play an active role in world affairs, remembering that the world exemplifies virtue and right action. Thus, moral worth, duty, and justice are singularly Stoic emphases, together with a certain sternness of mind. For the moral person neither is merciful nor shows pity, because each suggests a deviation from duty and from the fated necessity that rules the world. Nonetheless—with its loftiness of spirit and its emphasis on humanity's essential worth—the themes of universal brotherhood and the benevolence of divine nature make Stoicism one of the most appealing of philosophies.

Stoicism enabled the individual to better order his own life and to avoid the excesses of human nature that promote disquietude and anxiety. It was easily the most influential of the schools from the time of its founding through the first two centuries CE, and it continued to have a marked effect on later thought. During the late Roman and medieval periods, elements of Stoic moral theory were known and used in the formulation of Christian, Jewish, and Muslim theories of humanity and nature, of the state and society, and of law and sanctions — for example, in the works of Marcus Tullius Cicero (106–43 BCE), Roman statesman and orator; in Lactantius (240–320 CE), often called the "Christian Cicero"; and in Boethius (c. 470–524 CE), a scholar transitional to the Middle Ages. In the Renaissance, Stoic political and moral theory became more popular to theorists of natural law and political authority and of educational reform — for example, in Hugo Grotius (1583–1645), a Dutch jurist and statesman, and in Philipp Melanchthon (1497–1560), a major Reformation scholar. In the 20th century, Stoicism became popular again for its insistence on the value of the individual and the place of value in a world of strife and uncertainty — for example, in existentialism and in neo-orthodox Protestant theology.

EARLY GREEK STOICISM

After the death of Alexander the Great (323 BCE) and the partition of his empire into hereditary kingdoms, the greatness of the life and thought of the Greek city-state (polis) ended. With Athens no longer the political centre of the Mediterranean world, its claim to urbanity and cultural prominence passed on to other cities: Rome, Alexandria, and Pergamum. The Greek polis gave way to larger political units, and local rule was replaced by that of distant

Chrysippus of Soli discussed virtually every feature of Stoic doctrine and treated each so meticulously that the school's essential features scarcely changed after his time. The Bridgeman Art Library/Getty Images

governors. The earlier intimacy of order, cosmic and civic, was now replaced by social and political disorder. Traditional mores gave way to uncertain and transient values.

Stoicism had its beginnings in a changing world, in which earlier codes of conduct and ways of understanding proved no longer suitable. But it was also influenced by tenets of the older schools. The earliest Greek philosophers, the Milesians, had called attention to cosmic order and the beauty of nature. Later, the monist Parmenides (born *c.* 515 BCE) stressed the power of reason and thought, whereas Heracleitus (*c.* 540–*c.* 480 BCE), precursor of the philosophy of becoming, had alluded to the constancy of change and the omnipresence of divine fire, which illumined all things. A deeper understanding of human nature came with Socrates, who personified *sophia* and *sapientia* (Greek and Latin: "wisdom"). Of the several schools of philosophy stemming from Socrates, the Cynic and Megarian schools were influential in the early development of Stoic doctrine: the Cynics for their emphasis on the simple life, unadorned and free of emotional involvement; and the Megarians for their study of dialectic, logical form, and paradoxes.

Stoicism takes its name from the place where its founder, Zeno of Citium (*c.* 335–*c.* 263 BCE), customarily lectured— the Stoa Poikile (Painted Colonnade). Zeno was apparently well versed in Platonic thought, for he had studied at Plato's Academy both with Xenocrates of Chalcedon and with Polemon of Athens, successive heads of the Academy. Zeno established the central Stoic doctrines in logic, physics, and ethics, so that later Stoics were to expand rather than to change radically the views of the founder.

Zeno thus provided the following themes as the essential framework of Stoic ethics: human happiness as a product of life according to nature; physical theory as providing the means by which right actions are to be determined; the wise person as the model of human excellence; belief in the fated causality that necessarily binds all things; cosmopolitanism, or cultural outlook transcending narrower loyalties; and the human obligation, or duty, to choose only those acts that are in accord with nature, all other acts being a matter of indifference.

Cleanthes of Assos (*c.* 331–*c.* 232 BCE), who succeeded Zeno as head of the school, is best known for his *Hymn to Zeus,* which movingly describes Stoic reverence for the cosmic order and the power of universal reason and law. The third head of the school, Chrysippus of Soli (*c.* 280–*c.* 206 BCE), was perhaps the greatest and certainly the most productive of the early Stoics. Chrysippus was responsible for the attempt to show that fate and free will are not mutually exclusive conceptual features of Stoic doctrine. Zeno's view of the origin of human beings as providentially generated by "fiery reason" out of matter was expanded by Chrysippus to include the concept of self-preservation, which governs all living things. Another earlier view (Zeno's), that of nature as a model for life, was amplified first by Cleanthes and then by Chrysippus. The Zenonian appeal to life "according to nature" had evidently been left vague, because to Cleanthes it seemed necessary to speak of life in accord with nature conceived as the world at large (the cosmos), whereas Chrysippus distinguished between world nature and human nature. Thus, to do good is to act in accord with both human and universal nature.

He also established firmly that logic and (especially) physics are necessary and are means for the differentiation of goods and evils. Thus, a knowledge of physics (or theology) is required before an ethics can be formulated. Indeed, physics and logic find their value chiefly in this very purpose. Chrysippus covered almost every feature of Stoic doctrine and treated each so thoroughly that the essential features of the school were to change relatively little after his time.

LATER ROMAN STOICISM

The Middle Stoa, which flourished in the 2nd and early 1st centuries BCE, was dominated chiefly by Panaetius (*c.* 180–109 BCE), its founder, and his disciple Poseidonius (*c.* 135–*c.* 51 BCE), both from the Greek island of Rhodes. Panaetius organized a Stoic school in Rome before returning to Athens, and Poseidonius was largely responsible for an emphasis on the religious features of the doctrine. Both were antagonistic to the ethical doctrines of Chrysippus, who, they believed, had strayed too far from the Platonic and Aristotelian roots of Stoicism. It may have been because of the considerable time that Panaetius and Poseidonius lived in Rome that the Stoa there turned so much of its emphasis to the moral and religious themes within the Stoic doctrine. Panaetius was highly regarded by Cicero, who used him as a model for his own work.

Poseidonius, who had been a disciple of Panaetius in Athens, taught Cicero at his school at Rhodes and later went to Rome and remained there for a time with Cicero. If Poseidonius admired Plato and Aristotle, he was particularly interested—unlike most of his school—in the study of natural and providential phenomena. In presenting the Stoic system in the second book of *De natura deorum* (45 BCE), Cicero most probably followed Poseidonius. Because his master, Panaetius, was chiefly concerned with concepts of duty and obligation, it was his studies that served as a model for the *De officiis* (44 BCE) of Cicero. Hecaton, another of Panaetius's students and an active Stoic philosopher, also stressed similar ethical themes.

Panaetius and Poseidonius were chiefly responsible for the widespread popularity of Stoicism in Rome.

Bronze equestrian statue of Marcus Aurelius, in the Piazza del Campidoglio,
Rome, c. 173 CE. Height 5.03 m. Alinari—Art Resource/EB Inc.

It was precisely their turning of doctrine to themes in moral philosophy and natural science that appealed to the intensely practical Romans. The times perhaps demanded such interests, and with them Stoicism was to become predominantly a philosophy for the individual, showing how—given the vicissitudes of life—one might be stoical. Law, world citizenship, nature, and the benevolent workings of Providence and the divine reason were the principal areas of interest of Stoicism at this time.

These tendencies toward practicality are also well illustrated in the later period of the school (in the first two centuries CE) in the writings of Lucius Seneca (c. 4 BCE–65 CE), a Roman statesman; of Epictetus (c. 55–c. 135 CE), a former slave; and of Marcus Aurelius (121– 180 CE), a Roman emperor. Both style and content in the *Libri morales* (*Moral Essays*) and *Epistulae morales* (*Moral Letters*) of Seneca reinforce the new direction in Stoic thought. The *Encheiridion* (*Manual*) of Epictetus and the *Meditations* of Marcus Aurelius furthered the sublime and yet personal consolation of the Stoic message and increasingly showed the strength of its rivalry to the burgeoning power of the new Christianity.

The discussions of nature by St. Paul the Apostle, as in I Corinthians 11:14, may well have had Stoic beginnings. SuperStock/Getty Images

Logos

Logos, a concept of ancient Greek philosophy and theology, is the divine reason that is implicit in the cosmos, giving it order, form, and meaning. It became particularly significant in Christian writings and doctrines to describe or define the role of Jesus Christ.

The idea of the *logos* harks back at least to the 6th-century-BCE philosopher Heracleitus, who discerned in the cosmic process a *logos* analogous to the reasoning power in human beings. Later, the Stoics defined the *logos* as an active rational principle that permeated all reality. Philo of Alexandria, a 1st-century-CE Jewish philosopher, taught that the *logos* was the intermediary between God and the cosmos, being both the agent of creation and the agent through which the human mind can apprehend and comprehend God. According to Philo and the Middle Platonists (philosophers who interpreted in religious terms the teachings of Plato), the *logos* was both immanent in the world and at the same time the transcendent divine mind.

In the first chapter of The Gospel According to John, Jesus Christ is identified as "the Word" (*logos*) made flesh. This identification is based on concepts of revelation appearing in the Hebrew Bible (Old Testament), as in the frequently used phrase "the Word of the Lord," which connoted ideas of God's activity and power. The author of The Gospel According to John used the expression "the Word" to emphasize the redemptive character of the person of Christ, whom the author also describes as "the way, and the truth, and the life." Just as the Jews had viewed the Torah (the Law) as preexistent with God, so also the author of John viewed Jesus, but Jesus came to be regarded as the personified source of life and illumination of humankind. The author of John interprets the *logos* as inseparable from the person of Jesus and does not imply that it is simply the revelation that Jesus proclaims.

The identification of Jesus with the *logos* was further developed on the basis of Greek philosophical ideas in support of attempts by early Christian theologians to express the Christian faith in terms that would be intelligible to the Hellenistic world. Thus, in their apologies and polemical works, the early Christian Fathers stated that Christ as the preexistent *logos* (1) reveals the Father to humankind and is the subject of the Hebrew Bible manifestations of God; (2) is the divine reason in which the whole human race shares; and (3) is the divine will and word by which the worlds were framed.

Jesus Before the Gates of Jerusalem, *manuscript illumination by Liberale da Verona, 1470–74; in the Piccolomini Library, Siena, Italy.* SCALA/Art Resource, New York

STOIC ELEMENTS IN EARLY CHRISTIAN THOUGHT

There is much disagreement as to the measure of Stoic influence on the writings of St. Paul the Apostle (c. 4 BCE–c. 62 CE). At Tarsus, Paul certainly had opportunities for hearing Stoic lectures on philosophy. And it may be that his discussion of nature and the teaching of it (I Corinthians 11:14) is Stoic in origin, for it has a parallel in the *Manual* of Epictetus. Although not a Stoic technical term, *syneidēsis,* which Paul used as "conscience," was generally employed by Stoic philosophers. In I Corinthians 13 and in the report of Paul's speech at Athens (Acts 17), there is much that is Hellenistic, more than a little tinged by Stoic elements (e.g., the arguments concerning humans' natural belief in God and the belief that humans' existence is in God).

The assimilation of Stoic elements by the Church Fathers (the eminent bishops and teachers of early Christianity) was generally better understood by the 4th century. Stoic influence can be seen, for example, in the relation between reason and the passions in the works of St. Ambrose (339–397), one of the great scholars of the church, and of Marcus Minucius Felix (died c. 250), one of the earliest Christian Apologists to write in Latin. Each took a wealth of ideas from Stoic morality as Cicero had interpreted it in *De officiis.* In general, whereas the emerging Christian morality affirmed its originality, it also assimilated much of the pagan literature, the more congenial elements of which were essentially Stoic.

Earlier, in the 3rd century, Quintus Tertullian (c. 155–c. 220), often called the father of Latin Christian literature, seems to have been versed in Stoic philosophy—for example, in his theory of the agreement between the supernatural and the human soul, in his use of the Stoic tenet that from a truth there follow truths, and in his employment of the idea of universal consent. Even in his polemical writings, which reveal an unrelenting hostility to pagan philosophy, Tertullian showed a fundamental grasp and appreciation of such Stoic themes as the world *logos* and the relation of body to soul. This is well illustrated in his argument against the Stoics, particularly on their theme that God is a corporeal being and identified with reason as inherent in matter—also to be found in his polemics against Marcion (fl. 2nd century CE), father of a heretical Christian sect, and against Hermogenes of Tarsus (*c.* 160–225), author of an important digest of rhetoric. Yet in his doctrine of the Word, he appealed directly to Zeno and Cleanthes of the Early Stoa. Another important polemic against the Stoics is found in the treatise *Contra Celsum*, by Origen (*c.* 185–*c.* 254), the most influential Greek theologian of the 3rd century, in which he argued at some length against Stoic doctrines linking God to matter.

Also, St. Cyprian (200–258), bishop of Carthage, revealed the currency of Stoic views (e.g., in his *Ad Demetrianum*, a denunciation of an enemy to Christianity, in which Cyprian castigates the ill treatment of slaves, who, no less than their masters, are formed of the same matter and endowed with the same soul and live according to the same law). The beliefs in human brotherhood and in the world as a great city, commonly found in early Christian literature, were current Stoic themes. The Christian attitude appears in what St. Paul said of Baptism: "You are all sons of God through Faith. For as many of you as were baptized into Christ have put on Christ" (Galatians 3:26–27).

CONSEQUENTIALISM

Consequentialism is a theory of morality that derives duty or moral obligation from what is good or desirable as an end to be achieved. Also known as teleological ethics (from ancient Greek *telos*, "end"; *logos*, "reason"), it is often contrasted with deontological ethics (*deon*, "duty"), or deontology, which holds that the basic standards for an action's being morally right are independent of the good or evil generated. Modern normative ethics, especially since the deontological theory of the German philosopher Immanuel Kant (1724–1804), has been deeply divided between a form of consequentialism (utilitarianism) and various forms of deontology. Deontology will be discussed in detail in Chapter 2.

Consequentialist theories differ on the nature of the end that actions ought to promote. Utilitarian-type theories hold that the end consists in an experience or feeling produced by the action. Epicureanism, for example, taught that this feeling is pleasure, including especially the pleasures derived from friendship. Later theories based on pleasure included the utilitarianism of the English philosophers Jeremy Bentham (1748–1832), John Stuart Mill (1806–73), and Henry Sidgwick (1838–1900), with its formula the "greatest happiness [pleasure] of the greatest number." Many other consequentialist or utilitarian-type theories have been proposed, though none has been as influential as classical utilitarianism. For example, according to "evolutionary ethics," which originated with the English sociologist and philosopher Herbert Spencer (1820–1903) and was revived in the late 20th century, the proper end of action is survival and growth. According to some scholars, the Italian political philosopher Niccolò Machiavelli (1469–1527) and the German philosopher Friedrich Nietzsche (1844–1900) shared the view that right actions are directed toward the experience of power, as in despotism. Other theories favoured satisfaction and adjustment—as in the pragmatism of the American philosophers Ralph Barton

Perry (1876–1957) and John Dewey (1859–1952)—or free-dom, as in the existentialism of the French philosopher Jean-Paul Sartre (1905–80).

The chief problem for utilitarian theories has been to answer the conventional objection that ends do not always justify means. The problem arises in these theories because they tend to separate the achieved ends from the action by which these ends are produced. One implication of utilitarianism is that one's intention in performing an act may include all of its foreseen consequences. The goodness of the intention then reflects the balance of the good and evil of these consequences, with no limits imposed upon it by the nature of the act itself—even if it be, say, the break-ing of a promise or the execution of an innocent person. Utilitarianism, in answering this charge, must show either that what is apparently immoral is not really so or that, if it really is so, then closer examination of the consequences will bring this fact to light. Ideal utilitarianism, a view defended by the English philosopher G.E. Moore (1873–1958), tried to meet the difficulty by advocating a plurality of ends and including among them the attainment of virtue itself, which, as Mill affirmed, "may be felt a good in itself, and desired as such with as great intensity as any other good."

EPICUREANISM

In a strict sense, Epicureanism is the philosophy taught by Epicurus (341–270 BCE). In a broad sense, however, it is a system of ethics embracing every conception or form of life that can be traced to the principles of his philosophy. In ancient polemics, as often since, the term was employed with an even more generic (and clearly erroneous) mean-ing as the equivalent of a crude hedonism, according to which sensual pleasure is the chief good.

THE NATURE OF EPICUREANISM

Several fundamental concepts characterize the ethics of Epicurus. The basic concepts are the identification of good with pleasure and of the supreme good and ultimate end with the absence of pain from the body and the soul— a limit beyond which pleasure does not grow but changes; the reduction of every human relation to the principle of utility, which finds its highest expression in friendship, in which it is at the same time surmounted; and, in accordance with this end, the limitation of all desire and the practice of the virtues, from which pleasure is inseparable, and a withdrawn and quiet life.

In principle, Epicurus's ethic of pleasure is the exact opposite of the Stoic's ethic of duty. The consequences, however, are the same: in the end, the Epicurean is forced to live with the same temperance and justice as the Stoic. Of utmost importance, however, is one point of divergence: the walls of the Stoic's city are those of the world, and its law is that of reason; the limits of the Epicurean's city are those of a garden, and the law is that of friendship. Although this garden can also reach the boundaries of earth, its centre is always a human being.

HISTORY OF EPICUREANISM

Epicurus is remarkable for his systematic spirit and the unity that he tried to give to every part of philosophy. In this respect, he was greatly influenced by the philosophy and teachings of Aristotle—taking over the essentials of his doctrines and pursuing the problems that he posed.

In the Middle Ages Epicurus was known through Cicero and the polemics of the Church Fathers. To be an Epicurean at the time of the Italian poet and philosopher Dante (1265–1321) meant to be one who denied Providence and the immortality of the soul. The first modern defense

of Epicureanism was written by the notable human-
ist Lorenzo Valla (1407–57). In the dialogue *De voluptate*
(1431; "On Pleasure"), he maintained that the true good is
pleasure and not virtue but concluded that the supreme
pleasure is that which awaits the individual in heaven.
In terms of attitude and direction of thought, the first
two great Epicureans of the Renaissance were Michel de
Montaigne (1533–92) in France and Francesco Guicciardini
(1483–1540) in Italy. Epicurean in everything, as man and as
poet, was the early classicist Ludovico Ariosto (1474–1533).
But not until the French abbot Pierre Gassendi (1592–1655)
was the system of Epicurus to rise again in its entirety—
this time, however, by approaching truth through faith.
Gassendi in 1649 wrote a commentary on a book by the
3rd-century-CE biographer Diogenes Laërtius. This com-
ment, called the *Syntagma philosophiae Epicuri* ("Treatise
on Epicurean Philosophy"), was issued posthumously at
The Hague 10 years later. At the same time, in England,
Thomas Hobbes, a friend of Gassendi, took up again the
theory of pleasure and interpreted it in a dynamic sense.
Starting from the premise that, in the natural state, "man
is a wolf to man," he concluded that peace, without which
there is no happiness, cannot be guaranteed by anything
but force, and that this force must be relinquished, by
common agreement, to the power of only one.

During the 17th and 18th centuries, the European
country in which Epicureanism was most active was
France, where its representatives were called "liber-
tines," among them moralists such as François, duc de La
Rochefoucauld (1613–80) and scientists such as Julien de
La Mettrie (1709–51), who believed that humans could
be explained as machines; Claude-Adrien Helvétius
(1715–71), who reduced the ethic of the useful to a form
of experimental science but who put public above private
well-being; and Paul Henri Dietrich, baron d'Holbach

(1723–89), who gave particular importance to the physics of the atoms. The purely sensistic conception of knowledge had its most thoroughgoing theoretician in Étienne de Condillac (1715–80). In England, Adam Smith (1723–90), developing the ethical concepts of David Hume (1711–76), surmounted the egoism that is the basis of every act by using the principle of the impartial observer invoked to sympathize with one or another of the antagonists. After him, Jeremy Bentham, eliminating sympathy, reduced ethics to the pure calculus of the useful, which—in an entirely Epicurean formula—he defined as a "moral arithmetic." In the Epicurean stream lay also the utilitarianism of the 19th century, of which the greatest representative was John Stuart Mill.

The interpretation of pleasure as a psychic principle of action was initiated by Gustav Fechner (1801–87), the founder of psychophysics, and developed toward the end of the century by Sigmund Freud (1856–1939) on the psychoanalytic level of the unconscious.

Epicureanism and egocentric hedonism had few faithful representatives among 20th-century philosophers, though the viewpoint remained as a residue in some strains of popular thinking.

EPICURUS'S LIFE AND TEACHINGS

In 306 BCE, Epicurus established his school at Athens in his garden. The school thus came to be known as the Garden.

His Works

In accordance with the goal that he assigned to philosophy, Epicurus's teaching had a dogmatic character, in substance if not in form. He called his treatises *dialogismoi,* or "conversations." Because the utility of the doctrines lay in their application, he summarized them in *stoicheia,* or "elementary propositions," to be memorized. In this respect, Epicurus was the inventor of the catechetical method. The number of works produced by Epicurus and his disciples reveals an impressive theoretical activity. But no less important was the practical action in living by the virtues taught by him and in honouring the obligations of reciprocal help in the name of friendship. In these endeavours, continuous assistance was rendered by Epicurus himself, who, even when old and ill, was occupied in writing letters of admonishment, guidance, and comfort—everywhere announcing his gospel of peace and, under the name of pleasure, inviting to love.

His Ethical Doctrine

Philosophy was, for Epicurus, the art of living, and it aimed at the same time both to assure happiness and to supply means to achieve it. As for science, Epicurus was concerned only with the practical end in view. If possible, he would have done without it. "If we were not troubled by our suspicions of the phenomena of the sky and about death," he wrote, "and also by our failure to grasp the limits of pain and desires, we should have no need of natural science."

But this science requires a principle that guarantees its possibilities and its certainty and a method of constructing it. This principle and this method are the object of the "Canon," which Epicurus substituted for Logic. Since he made the "Canon" an integral introduction to the "Physics," however, his philosophy falls into two parts, the "Physics" and the "Ethics."

As part of his "Physics," Epicurus's psychology held that the soul must be a body. It is made of very thin atoms of four different species—motile, quiescent, igneous, and ethereal—the last, thinnest and the most mobile of all, serving to explain sensitivity and thought. Thus constituted, the soul is, from another perspective, bipartite: in part distributed throughout the entire body and in part collected in the chest. The first part is the locus of sensations and of the physical affects of pain and pleasure; the second (entirely dissociated from the first) is the *psyche* par excellence—the seat of thought, emotions, and will. Thought is caused not by the transmission of sense motion but by the perception of images constituted by films that continuously issue from all bodies and, retaining their form, arrive at the *psyche* through the pores. The full autonomy and freedom of the *psyche* is assured, as, with an act of apprehension, it seizes at every moment the images it needs, meanwhile remaining master of its own feelings.

The object of ethics is to determine the end and the means necessary to reach it. Taking his cue from experience, Epicurus looked to the animal kingdom for his answer. He concluded from this cue that the chief end is pleasure. He distinguished two kinds—a "kinetic" pleasure of sense and a "static" pleasure, consisting in the absence of pain—and taught that the pleasure of sense is good, though it is not good merely as motion but rather as a motion favourable to the nature of the receiving sense organ. In essence, pleasure is the equilibrium of the being with itself, existing wherever there is no pain.

Epicurus concluded that "freedom from pain in the body and from trouble in the mind" is the ultimate aim of a happy life. The damages and the advantages following the realization of any desire must be measured in a calculus in which even pain must be faced with courage if the consequent pleasure will be of longer duration.

Having thus given order to his life, however, the wise person must also provide himself with security. This he achieves in two ways: by reducing his needs to a minimum and withdrawing, far from human competition and from the noise of the world, to "live hidden"; and by adding the private compact of friendship to the public compact from which laws arise. To be sure, friendship stems from utility; but, once born, it is desirable in itself. Epicurus then added that "for love of friendship one has even to put in jeopardy love itself"; for every existence, being alone, needs the other. "To eat and drink without a friend," he wrote, "is to devour like the lion and the wolf." Thus, the utility sublimates itself and changes into love. But as every love is intrepid, the wise person, "if his friend is put to torture, suffers as if he himself were there" and, if necessary, "will die for his friend." Thus, into the bloody world of his time, Epicurus could launch the cry: "Friendship runs dancing through the world bringing to us all the summons to wake and sing its praises."

If human unhappiness stemmed only from vain desires and worldly dangers, this wisdom, founded upon prudence alone, would suffice. But besides these sources of unhappiness there are two great fears, fear of death and fear of the gods. If science, however, is effective in revealing the bounds of desire and in quelling the fear of the gods, it can also allay the fear of death. Regarding the soul as a body within another body, science envisions it as dissolving when the body dissolves. Death, then, "is nothing to us, so long as we exist, death is not with us; but when death comes, then we do not exist." But death is feared not only for what may be waiting in the beyond but also for itself. "I am not afraid of being dead," said the comic poet Epicharmus of Cos (c. 530–c. 440 BCE), "I just do not want to die." The very idea of not existing instills a fear that Epicurus considered to be the cause of all the passions that pain the soul and disorder people's lives. Against it Epicurus argued that if pleasure is perfect within each instant and "infinite time contains no greater pleasure than limited time, if one measures by reason the limits of pleasure," then all desire of immortality is vain. Thus, Epicurus's most distinguished pupil, Metrodorus of Lampsacus (331–278 BCE), could exclaim, *"bebiōtai"* ("I have lived"), and this would be quite enough. He who has conquered the fear of death can also despise pain, which "if it is long lasting is light, and if it is intense is short" and brings death nearer. The wise person has only to replace the image of pain present in the flesh with that of blessings enjoyed, and he can be happy even "inside the bull of Phalaris." The most beautiful example was set by Epicurus at the moment of his death:

A happy day is this on which I write to you.... The pains which I feel...could not be greater. But all of this is opposed by the happiness which the soul experiences, remembering our conversations of a bygone time.

The ultimate concentration of all his wisdom is the *Tetrapharmacon,* preserved by Philodemus (110–35 BCE): "The gods are not to be feared. Death is not a thing that one must fear. Good is easy to obtain. Evil is easy to tolerate."

The Epicurean School

Epicurus's successor in the direction of the Garden was Hermarchus of Mytilene, and he was succeeded in turn by Polystratus, who was the last survivor to have heard Epicurus. Superior to both, however, were Metrodorus and Colotes, against whom a small work by Plutarch (46–c. 120 CE) was directed. Among the Epicureans of the 2nd century BCE, mention must be made of Demetrius of Lacon, of whose works some fragments remain, and Apollodorus, who wrote more than 400 books. Much was also written by his disciple Zeno of Sidon, who was heard by Cicero in 79 BCE in Athens. After Zeno, there were Phaedrus, also a teacher of Cicero, who was in Rome in 90 BCE, and Patro, the head of the school until 51 BCE. Already famous as an epigram writer was Philodemus of Gadara (born 110 BCE).

In the papyri of Herculaneum, comprising the effects of Philodemus's library, there are sizable remains of almost all of his numerous works.

Epicureanism had already been introduced in Rome, in the 2nd century BCE. The first person to spread its doctrines in Latin prose was a certain Amafinius. At the time of Cicero, Epicureanism was in fact the philosophy in vogue, and according to Cicero the number of Romans subscribing to it was considerable. Among the greatest Epicureans was Titus Lucretius Carus (c. 95–55 BCE), who, in the poem *De rerum natura* ("On the Nature of Things"), left an almost complete and amazingly precise exposition of Epicurus's "Physics." The extent to which Epicurus was still popular in the 1st century after Christ is demonstrated by Seneca, who cited and defended him. To the 2nd century CE belongs Diogenes of Oenoanda, who carved Epicurus's works on a portico wall. In the same century should perhaps be mentioned Diogenianus, fragments of whose polemic against the Stoic Chrysippus are found in the church historian Eusebius. Also Epicurean, between the 4th and 5th centuries, was the epigrammatist Palladas.

On account of its dogmatic character and its practical end, the philosophy of Epicurus was not subject to development, except in the polemic and in its application to themes that Epicurus either had treated briefly or had never dealt with at all. To be aware of this, it is sufficient to run through what remains of the representatives of his school and particularly of the works of Philodemus of Gadara. Epicurus's philosophy remained essentially unchanged. Once truth has been found, it requires no more discussion, particularly when it completely satisfies the end toward which human nature tends. The main thing is to see this end; all of the rest comes by itself, and there is no longer anything to do but follow Epicurus, "liberator" and "saviour," and to memorize his "oracular words."

UTILITARIANISM

Utilitarianism is an ethical theory according to which an action is right if it tends to promote happiness and wrong if it tends to promote unhappiness—not only for the agent but also for everyone affected. Thus, utilitarians focus on the consequences of an act rather than on its intrinsic nature or the motives of the agent. Classical utilitarianism is hedonist, but values other than, or in addition to, pleasure (as in ideal utilitarianism) can be employed, or—more neutrally, and in a version popular in economics—anything can be regarded as valuable that appears as an object of rational or informed desire (as in preference utilitarianism). The test of utility maximization can also be applied directly to single acts (act utilitarianism), or to acts only indirectly through some other suitable object of moral assessment, such as rules of conduct (rule utilitarianism).

Utilitarianism is in opposition to egoism, the view that a person should pursue his own self-interest, even at the expense of others, and to any ethical theory that regards some acts or types of acts as right or wrong independently of their consequences. Utilitarianism also differs from ethical theories that make the rightness or wrongness of an act dependent upon the motive of the agent; for, according to the utilitarian, it is possible for the right thing to be done from a bad motive.

BASIC CONCEPTS

The utilitarian understands the consequences of an action to include all of the good and bad produced, whether arising after the action has been performed or during its performance. If the difference in the consequences of alternative actions is not great, some utilitarians do not regard the choice between them as a moral issue. According to John Stuart Mill, actions should be classified

Jeremy Bentham, detail of an oil painting by H.W. Pickersgill, 1829; in the National Portrait Gallery, London. Courtesy of the National Portrait Gallery, London

as morally right or wrong only if the consequences are of such significance that a person would wish to see the agent compelled, not merely persuaded and exhorted, to act in the preferred manner.

In assessing the consequences of actions, utilitarianism relies on some theory of intrinsic value: something is held to be good in itself, apart from further consequences, and all other values are believed to derive their worth from their relation to this intrinsic good as a means to an end. Jeremy Bentham and Mill were hedonists; that is, they analyzed happiness as a balance of pleasure over pain and believed that these feelings alone are of intrinsic value and disvalue. Utilitarians also assume that it is possible to compare the intrinsic values produced by two alternative actions and to estimate which would have better consequences. Bentham believed that a "hedonic calculus" is theoretically possible. A moralist, he maintained, could sum up the units of pleasure and the units of pain for everyone likely to be affected, immediately and in the future, and could take the balance as a measure of the overall good or evil tendency of an action. Such precise measurement as Bentham envisioned is perhaps not essential, but it is nonetheless necessary for the utilitarian to make some interpersonal comparisons of the values of the effects of alternative courses of action.

METHODOLOGIES

As a normative system providing a standard by which an individual ought to act and by which the existing practices of society, including its moral code, ought to be evaluated and improved, utilitarianism cannot be verified or confirmed in the way in which a descriptive theory can. But it is not regarded by its exponents as simply arbitrary. Bentham believed that only in terms of a utilitarian interpretation do words such as "ought," "right," and "wrong" have meaning and that whenever anyone attempts to combat the principle of utility, he does so with reasons drawn from the principle itself. Bentham and Mill both believed that human actions are motivated entirely by pleasure and pain. Mill saw that motivation as a basis for the argument that, because happiness is the sole end of human action, the promotion of happiness is the test by which to judge all human conduct.

One of the leading utilitarians of the late 19th century, Cambridge philosopher Henry Sidgwick, rejected their theories of motivation as well as Bentham's theory of the meaning of moral terms and sought to support utilitarianism by showing that it follows from systematic reflection on the morality of "common sense." Most of the requirements of commonsense morality, he argued, could be based on utilitarian considerations. In addition, he reasoned that utilitarianism could solve the difficulties and perplexities that arise from the vagueness and inconsistencies of commonsense doctrines.

CRITICISMS

Most opponents of utilitarianism have held that it has implications contrary to their moral intuitions—that considerations of utility, for example, might sometimes sanction the breaking of a promise. Much of the defense of utilitarian ethics has consisted in answering these objections, either by showing that utilitarianism does not have the implications that they claim it has or by arguing against the moral intuitions of its opponents. Some utilitarians, however, have sought to modify the utilitarian theory to account for the objections.

One such criticism is that, although the widespread practice of lying and stealing would have bad consequences, resulting in a loss of trustworthiness and security, it is not certain that an occasional lie to avoid embarrassment or an occasional theft from a rich person would not have good consequences, and thus be permissible or even required by utilitarianism. But the utilitarian readily answers that the widespread practice of such acts would result in a loss of trustworthiness and security. To meet the objection to not permitting an occasional lie or theft, some philosophers have defended a modification labelled "rule" utilitarianism. It permits a particular act on a particular occasion to be judged right or wrong according to whether it is in accordance with or in violation of a useful rule. A rule is judged useful or not by the consequences of its general practice. Mill has sometimes been interpreted as a "rule" utilitarian, whereas Bentham and Sidgwick were "act" utilitarians.

Another objection, often posed against the hedonistic value theory held by Bentham, holds that the value of life is more than a balance of pleasure over pain. Mill, in contrast to Bentham, discerned differences in the quality of pleasures that made some intrinsically preferable to others independently of intensity and duration (the quantitative dimensions recognized by Bentham). Some philosophers in the utilitarian tradition have recognized certain wholly nonhedonistic values, such as beauty, without losing their utilitarian credentials.

Even in limiting the recognition of intrinsic value and disvalue to happiness and unhappiness, some philosophers have argued that those feelings cannot adequately be further broken down into terms of pleasure and pain and have thus preferred to defend the theory in terms of maximizing happiness and minimizing unhappiness. It is important to note, however, that even for the hedonistic utilitarians, pleasure and pain are not thought of in purely sensual terms. Pleasure and pain for them can be components of experiences of all sorts. Their claim is that, if an experience is neither pleasurable nor painful, then it is a matter of indifference and has no intrinsic value.

Another objection to utilitarianism is that the prevention or elimination of suffering should take precedence over any alternative action that would only increase the happiness of someone already happy. Some 20th-century utilitarians modified their theory to require this focus or even to limit moral obligation to the prevention or elimination of suffering—a view labelled "negative" utilitarianism.

HISTORICAL SURVEY

The ingredients of utilitarianism are found in the history of thought long before Bentham. A hedonistic theory of the value of life is found in the early 5th century BCE in the ethics of Aristippus of Cyrene (c. 435–366 BCE), founder of the Cyrenaic school, and 100 years later in that of Epicurus. The seeds of ethical universalism are found in the doctrines of the rival ethical school of Stoicism and in Christianity.

Growth of Classical English Utilitarianism

In the history of English philosophy, some historians have identified Bishop Richard Cumberland (1631–1718) as the first to have a utilitarian philosophy. A generation later, however, Francis Hutcheson (1694–1746), a Scots-Irish "moral sense" theorist, more clearly held a utilitarian view. He not only analyzed that action as best that "procures the greatest happiness for the greatest numbers" but proposed a form of "moral arithmetic" for calculating the best consequences. The Skeptic David Hume, Scotland's foremost philosopher and historian, attempted to analyze the origin of the virtues in terms of their contribution to utility. Bentham said that he discovered the principle of utility in the 18th-century writings of various thinkers: Joseph Priestley (1733–1804), a dissenting clergyman famous for his discovery of oxygen; Frenchman Claude-Adrien Helvétius (1715–71), author of a philosophy of mere sensation; Cesare Beccaria (1738–94), an Italian legal theorist; and Hume. Helvétius probably drew from Hume, and Beccaria from Helvétius.

Another strand of utilitarian thought took the form of a theological ethics. John Gay, a biblical scholar and philosopher, held the will of God to be the criterion of virtue. But from God's goodness he inferred that God willed that men promote human happiness.

Bentham, who apparently believed that an individual in governing his own actions would always seek to maximize his own pleasure and minimize his own pain, found in pleasure and pain both the cause of human action and the basis for a normative criterion of action. Bentham called the art of governing one's own actions "private ethics." The happiness of the agent is the determining factor. The happiness of others governs only to the extent that the agent is motivated by sympathy, benevolence, or interest in the good will and good opinion of others. For Bentham, the greatest happiness of the greatest number would play a role primarily in the art of legislation, in which the legislator would seek to maximize the happiness of the entire community by creating an identity of interests between each individual and his fellows. By laying down penalties for mischievous acts, the legislator would make it unprofitable for a person to harm his neighbour. Bentham's major philosophical work, *An Introduction to the Principles of Morals and Legislation* (1789), was designed as an introduction to a plan of a penal code.

With Bentham, utilitarianism became the ideological foundation of a reform movement, later known as "philosophical radicalism," that would test all institutions and policies by the principle of utility. Bentham attracted as

John Stuart Mill, 1884. Library of Congres, Neg. Co. LC-USZ62-76491

his disciples a number of younger (earlier 19th-century) thinkers. They included David Ricardo (1772–1823), who gave classical form to the science of economics; John Stuart Mill's father, James Mill (1773–1836); and John Austin (1790–1859), a legal theorist. James Mill argued for representative government and universal male suffrage on utilitarian grounds, and he and other followers of Bentham were advocates of parliamentary reform in England in the early 19th century. John Stuart Mill promoted women's suffrage, state-supported education for all, and other proposals that were considered radical in their day. He argued on utilitarian grounds for freedom of speech and expression and for the noninterference of government or society in individual behaviour that did not harm anyone else. His essay "Utilitarianism," published in *Fraser's Magazine* (1861), is an elegant defense of the general utilitarian doctrine and perhaps remains the best introduction to the subject. In it utilitarianism is viewed as an ethics for ordinary individual behaviour as well as for legislation.

Modern Varieties of Utilitarianism

By the time Sidgwick wrote, utilitarianism had become one of the foremost ethical theories of the day. His *Methods of Ethics* (1874), a comparative examination of egoism, the ethics of common sense, and utilitarianism, contains the most careful discussion to be found of the implications of utilitarianism as a principle of individual moral action.

The 20th century saw the development of various modifications and complications of the utilitarian theory. G.E. Moore, a pioneer of 20th-century analytic philosophy, regarded many kinds of experience—including love, knowledge, and the appreciation of beauty—as intrinsically valuable independently of pleasure, a position labelled "ideal" utilitarianism. He famously proposed that one imagine two universes in which there are equal quantities of pleasure but vastly different amounts of beauty. He thought it obvious that the more beautiful world is to be preferred. The recognition of "act" utilitarianism and "rule" utilitarianism as explicit alternatives was stimulated by the analysis of moral reasoning in "rule" utilitarian terms by the English philosophers Stephen Toulmin (1922–2009) and Patrick Nowell-Smith (1915–2006); the interpretation of Mill as a "rule" utilitarian by another English moralist, J.O. Urmson; and the analysis by John Rawls (1921–2002), an American political and moral philosopher, of the significance for utilitarianism of two different conceptions of moral rules. "Act" utilitarianism was defended by the Australian-born philosopher J.J.C. Smart, however.

EFFECTS OF UTILITARIANISM IN OTHER FIELDS

The influence of utilitarianism has been widespread, permeating the intellectual life of the last two centuries. Its significance in law, politics, and economics is especially notable.

The utilitarian theory of the justification of punishment stands in opposition to the "retributive" theory, according to which punishment is intended to make the criminal "pay" for his crime. According to the utilitarian, the rationale of punishment is entirely to prevent further crime by either reforming the criminal or protecting society from him and to deter others from crime through fear of punishment.

In its political philosophy, utilitarianism bases the authority of government and the sanctity of individual rights upon their utility, thus providing an alternative to theories of natural law, natural rights, or social contract. What kind of government is best thus becomes a question of what kind of government has the best consequences—an assessment that requires factual premises regarding human nature and behaviour.

Generally, utilitarians have supported democracy as a way of making the interest of government coincide with the general interest. They have argued for the greatest individual liberty compatible with an equal liberty for others on the ground that each individual is generally the best judge of his own welfare. And utilitarians have believed in the possibility and the desirability of progressive social change through peaceful political processes.

With different factual assumptions, however, utilitarian arguments can lead to different conclusions. If the inquirer assumes that a strong government is required to check humans' basically selfish interests and that any change may threaten the stability of the political order, he may be led by utilitarian arguments to an authoritarian or conservative position. In contrast, William Godwin (1756–1836), an English political philosopher, assumed the basic goodness of human nature and argued that the greatest happiness would follow from a radical alteration of society in the direction of anarchistic communism.

Classical economics received some of its most important statements from utilitarian writers, especially Ricardo and John Stuart Mill. Ironically, its theory of economic value was framed primarily in terms of the cost of labour in production rather than in terms of the use value, or utility, of commodities. Later developments more clearly reflected the utilitarian philosophy. William Jevons (1835–82), one of the founders of the marginal utility school of analysis, derived many of his ideas from Bentham. And "welfare economics," while substituting comparative preferences for comparative utilities, reflected the basic spirit of the utilitarian philosophy. In economic policy, the early utilitarians had tended to oppose governmental interference in trade and industry on the assumption that the economy would regulate itself for the greatest welfare if left alone. Later utilitarians lost confidence in the social efficiency of private enterprise, however, and were willing to see governmental power and administration used to correct its abuses.

As a movement for the reform of social institutions, 19th-century utilitarianism was remarkably successful in the long run. Most of utilitarian recommendations have since been implemented unless abandoned by the reformers themselves; and, equally important, utilitarian arguments are now commonly employed to advocate institutional or policy changes.

SUMMARY AND EVALUATION

As an abstract ethical doctrine, utilitarianism has established itself as one of the small number of live options that must be taken into account and either refuted or accepted by any philosopher taking a position in normative ethics. In contemporary discussion it has been divorced from adventitious involvements with the analysis of ethical language and with the psychological theory with which it was presented by Bentham. Utilitarianism now appears in various modified and complicated formulations. Bentham's ideal of a hedonic calculus is usually considered a practical if not a theoretical impossibility. Present-day philosophers have noticed further problems in the utilitarian procedures. One of them, for example, is with the process of identifying the consequences of an act—a process that raises conceptual as well as practical problems as to what are to be counted as consequences, even without precisely quantifying the value of those consequences. The question may arise whether the outcome of an election is a consequence of each and every vote cast for the winning candidate if he receives more than the number necessary for election; and in estimating the value of the consequences, one may ask whether the entire value or only a part of the value of the outcome of the election is to be assigned to each vote. There is also difficulty in the procedure of comparing alternative acts. If one act requires a longer period of time for its performance than another, one may ask whether they can be considered alternatives. Even what is to count as an act is not a matter of philosophical consensus.

These problems, however, are common to almost all normative ethical theories, since most of them recognize the consequences—including the hedonic—of an act as being relevant ethical considerations. The central insight of utilitarianism, that one ought to promote happiness and prevent unhappiness whenever possible, seems undeniable. The critical question, however, is whether the whole of normative ethics can be analyzed in terms of this simple formula.

CHAPTER 2

NORMATIVE ETHICS: CONTRACTUALISM, DEONTOLOGY, FEMINISM, AND EGOISM

Since at least the 17th century, utilitarian ethical theories have been forcefully opposed by various forms of contractualism (also called social-contract theory) and deontology. Egoism, which also dates from the 17th century, has lost much of its early appeal among moral philosophers but has been defended by some modern students of economics and politics as a natural extension of the doctrine of laissez-faire. Beginning in the second half of the 20th century, philosophical feminism challenged traditional concepts and methods in many areas of philosophy, especially ethics.

CONTRACTUALISM

The contractualist approach in normative ethics is based on the notion of the "social contract," which is conceived as an actual or hypothetical compact between the ruled and their rulers. The terms of the supposed contract are used as the basis of a justification of the political authority of the rulers, the rights of the ruled, or both. The original inspiration for the notion may derive from the biblical covenant between God and Abraham, but it is most closely associated with the writings of Thomas Hobbes (1588–1679), John Locke (1632–1704), and Jean-Jacques Rousseau (1712–78). John Rawls (1921–2002) was an influential social-contract theorist. The idea of the social contract influenced the shapers of the American and French revolutions and the constitutions that followed them.

THOMAS HOBBES

Thomas Hobbes presented his political philosophy in different forms for different audiences. His work *De Cive* (1642) states his theory in what he regarded as its most scientific form. Unlike *The Elements of Law* (1650), which was composed in English for English parliamentarians — and which was written with local political challenges to King Charles I in mind—*De Cive* was a Latin work for an audience of Continental savants who were interested in the "new" science—that is, the sort of science that did not appeal to the authority of the ancients but approached various problems with fresh principles of explanation.

De Cive's break from the ancient authority par excellence—Aristotle—could not have been more loudly advertised. After only a few paragraphs, Hobbes rejects one of the most famous theses of Aristotle's politics, namely that human beings are naturally suited to life in a polis (city-state) and do not fully realize their natures until they exercise the role of citizen. Hobbes turns Aristotle's claim on its head: human beings, he insists, are by nature unsuited to political life. They naturally denigrate and compete with each other, are too easily swayed by the rhetoric of ambitious men, and think much more highly of themselves than of other people. In short, their passions magnify the value they place on their own interests, especially their near-term interests. At the same time, most people, in pursuing their own interests, do not have the

ability to prevail over competitors. Nor can they appeal
to some natural common standard of behaviour by which
everyone will feel obliged to abide. There is no natural self-
restraint, even when human beings are moderate in their
appetites, for a ruthless and bloodthirsty few can make
even the moderate feel forced to take violent preemp-
tive action to avoid losing everything. The self-restraint
even of the moderate, then, easily turns into aggression.
In other words, no human being is above aggression and
the anarchy that goes with it.

War comes more naturally to human beings than political order. Indeed, political order is possible only when
human beings abandon their natural condition of judging
and pursuing what seems best to each and delegate this judgment to someone else. This delegation is effected when the
many form a social contract among themselves to submit to
a sovereign in return for physical safety and a modicum of
well-being. Each of the many in effect says to the other: "I
transfer my right of governing myself to X (the sovereign)
if you do too." And the transfer is collectively entered into
only on the understanding that it makes one less of a tar-
get of attack or dispossession than one would be in one's
natural state. Although Hobbes did not assume that there
was ever a real historical event in which a mutual promise
was made to delegate self-government to a sovereign, he
claimed that the best way to understand the state was to
conceive of it as having resulted from such an agreement.

In Hobbes's social contract, the many trade liberty for
safety. Liberty, with its standing invitation to local conflict
and finally all-out war—a "war of every man against every
man"—is overvalued in traditional political philosophy
and popular opinion, according to Hobbes. It is better for
people to transfer the right of governing themselves to the
sovereign. Once transferred, however, this right of government is absolute, unless the many feel that their lives

are threatened by submission. The sovereign determines who owns what, who will hold which public offices, how the economy will be regulated, what acts will be crimes, and what punishments criminals should receive. The sovereign is the supreme commander of the army, supreme interpreter of law, and supreme interpreter of scripture, with authority over any national church. It is unjust—a case of reneging on what one has agreed—for any subject to take issue with these arrangements, for, in the act of creating the state or by receiving its protection, one agrees to leave judgments about the means of collective well-being and security to the sovereign. The sovereign's laws and decrees and appointments to public office may be unpopular. They may even be wrong. But unless the sovereign fails so utterly that subjects feel that their condition would be no worse in the free-for-all outside the state, it is better for the subjects to endure the sovereign's rule.

It is better both prudentially and morally. Because no one can prudently welcome a greater risk of death, no one can prudently prefer total liberty to submission. Total liberty invites war, and submission is the best insurance against war. Morality too supports this conclusion, for, according to Hobbes, all the moral precepts enjoining virtuous behaviour can be understood as derivable from the fundamental moral precept that one should seek peace—that is to say, freedom from war—if it is safe to do so. Without peace, he observed, man lives in "continual fear, and danger of violent death," and what life he has is "solitary, poor, nasty, brutish, and short." What Hobbes calls the "laws of nature," the system of moral rules by which everyone is bound, cannot be safely complied with outside the state, for the total liberty that people have outside the state includes the liberty to flout the moral requirements if one's survival seems to depend on it.

The sovereign is not a party to the social contract. He receives the obedience of the many as a free gift in their hope that he will see to their safety. The sovereign makes no promises to the many to win their submission. Indeed, because he does not transfer his right of self-government to anyone, he retains the total liberty that his subjects trade for safety. He is not bound by law, including his own laws. Nor does he do anything unjustly if he makes decisions about his subjects's safety and well-being that they do not like.

Although the sovereign is in a position to judge the means of survival and well-being for the many more dispassionately than they are able to do themselves, he is not immune to self-interested passions. Hobbes realizes that the sovereign may behave iniquitously. He insists that it is particularly imprudent for a sovereign to act so iniquitously that he disappoints his subjects's expectation of safety and makes them feel insecure. Subjects who are in fear of their lives lose their obligations to obey and, with that, deprive the sovereign of his power. Reduced to the status of one among many by the defection of his subjects, the unseated sovereign is likely to feel the wrath of those who submitted to him in vain.

Hobbes's masterpiece, *Leviathan* (1651), does not significantly depart from the view of *De Cive* concerning the relation between protection and obedience, but it devotes much more attention to the civil obligations of Christian believers and the proper and improper roles of a church within a state. Hobbes argues that believers do not endanger their prospects of salvation by obeying a sovereign's decrees to the letter, and he maintains that churches do not have any authority that is not granted by the civil sovereign.

Hobbes's political views exerted a discernible influence on his work in other fields, including historiography and legal theory. His political philosophy is chiefly concerned with the way in which government must be organized to avoid civil war. It therefore encompasses a view of the typical causes of civil war, all of which are represented in

Behemoth; or, The Long Parliament (1679), his history of the English Civil Wars. Hobbes produced the first English translation of Thucydides' *History of the Pelopponesian War*, which he thought contained important lessons for his contemporaries regarding the excesses of democracy, the worst kind of dilution of sovereign authority, in his view.

Hobbes's works on church history and the history of philosophy also strongly reflect his politics. He was firmly against the separation of government powers, either between branches of government or between church and state. His ecclesiastical history emphasizes the way in which power-hungry priests and popes threatened legitimate civil authority. His history of philosophy is mostly concerned with how metaphysics was used as a means of keeping people under the sway of Roman Catholicism at the expense of obedience to a civil authority. His theory of law develops a similar theme regarding the threats to a supreme civil power posed by common law and the multiplication of authoritative legal interpreters.

JOHN LOCKE

John Locke's importance as a political philosopher lies in the argument of the second of his *Two Treatises of Government* (1690). He begins by defining political power as a

> *right of making Laws with Penalties of Death, and consequently all less Penalties, for the Regulating and Preserving of Property, and of employing the force of the Community, in the Execution of such Laws and in defence of the Common-wealth from Foreign Injury, and all this only for the Publick Good.*

Much of the remainder of the *Treatise* is a commentary on this paragraph.

John Locke incorporated individualism within the structure of the law of nature and explained the origins and limits of legitimate government authority. Hulton Archive/Getty Images

THE STATE OF NATURE AND THE SOCIAL CONTRACT

Locke's definition of political power has an immediate moral dimension. It is a "right" of making laws and enforcing them for "the public good." Power for Locke never simply means "capacity" but always "morally sanctioned capacity." Morality pervades the whole arrangement of society, and it is this fact, tautologically, that makes society legitimate.

Locke's account of political society is based on a hypothetical consideration of the human condition before the beginning of communal life. In this "state of nature," humans are entirely free. But this freedom is not a state of complete license, because it is set within the bounds of the law of nature. It is a state of equality, which is itself a central element of Locke's account. In marked contrast to Sir Robert Filmer's world (see page 76), there is no natural hierarchy among humans. Each person is naturally free and equal under the law of nature, subject only to the will of "the infinitely wise Maker." Each person, moreover, is required to enforce as well as to obey this law. It is this duty that gives to humans the right to punish offenders. But in such a state of nature, it is obvious that placing the right to punish in each person's hands may lead to injustice and violence. This can be remedied if humans enter into a contract with each other to recognize by common consent a civil government with the power to enforce the law of nature among the citizens of that state. Although any contract is legitimate as long as it does not infringe upon the law of nature, it often happens that a contract can be enforced only if there is some higher human authority to require compliance with it. It is a primary function of society to set up the framework in which legitimate contracts, freely entered into, may be enforced, a state of affairs much more difficult to guarantee in the state of nature and outside civil society.

PROPERTY

Before discussing the creation of political society in greater detail, Locke provides a lengthy account of his notion of property, which is of central importance to his political theory. Each person, according to Locke, has property in his own person—that is, each person literally owns his own body. Other people may not use a person's body for any purpose without his permission. But one can acquire property beyond one's own body through labour. By mixing one's labour with objects in the world, one acquires a right to the fruits of that work. If one's labour turns a barren field into crops or a pile of wood into a house, the valuable product of that labour, the crops or the house, becomes one's property. Locke's view was a forerunner of the labour theory of value, which was expounded in different forms by the 19th-century economists David Ricardo (1772–1823) and Karl Marx (1818–83).

Clearly, each person is entitled to as much of the product of his labour as he needs to survive. But, according to Locke, in the state of nature one is not entitled to hoard surplus produce—one must share it with those less fortunate. God has "given the World to Men in common...to make use of to the best advantage of Life, and convenience." The introduction of money, while radically changing the economic base of society, was itself a contingent development, for money has no intrinsic value but depends for its utility only on convention.

Locke's account of property and how it comes to be owned faces difficult problems. For example, it is far from clear how much labour is required to turn any given unowned object into a piece of private property. In the case of a piece of land, for example, is it sufficient merely to put a fence around it? Or must it be plowed as well? There is, nevertheless, something intuitively powerful in the notion that it is activity, or work, that grants one a property right in something.

ORGANIZATION OF GOVERNMENT

Locke returns to political society in Chapter VIII of the second treatise. In the community created by the social contract, the will of the majority should prevail, subject to the law of nature. The legislative body is central, but it cannot create laws that violate the law of nature, because the enforcement of the natural law regarding life, liberty, and property is the rationale of the whole system. Laws must apply equitably to all citizens and not favour particular sectional interests, and there should be a division of legislative, executive, and judicial powers. The legislature may, with the agreement of the majority, impose such taxes as are required to fulfill the ends of the state—including, of course, its defense. If the executive power fails to provide the conditions under which the people can enjoy their rights under natural law, the people are entitled to remove him, by force if necessary. Thus, revolution, in extremis, is permissible—as Locke obviously thought it was in 1688–89, during the Glorious Revolution against King James II of England.

The significance of Locke's vision of political society can scarcely be exaggerated. His integration of individualism within the framework of the law of nature and his account of the origins and limits of legitimate government authority inspired the U.S. Declaration of Independence (1776) and the broad outlines of the system of government adopted in the U.S. Constitution. George Washington, the first president of the United States, once described Locke as "the greatest man who had ever lived." In France too, Lockean principles found clear expression in the Declaration of the Rights of Man and of the Citizen and other justifications of the French Revolution of 1789.

JEAN-JACQUES ROUSSEAU

Jean-Jacques Rousseau wrote two great works of political philosophy: the *Discours sur l'origine de l'inegalité* (1755; *Discourse on the Origin of Inequality*) and *Du Contrat social* (1762; *The Social Contract*). The former was written in response to a question posed by the Academy of Dijon, France: "What is the origin of the inequality among men and is it justified by natural law?" In response to this challenge he produced a masterpiece of speculative anthropology. The argument follows on that of the earlier *Discours sur les sciences et les arts* (1750; *A Discourse on the Sciences and the Arts*) by developing the proposition that humans in their natural state are good and then tracing the successive stages by which humans have descended from primitive innocence to corrupt sophistication.

Rousseau begins his *Discourse on the Origin of Inequality* by distinguishing two kinds of inequality, natural and artificial, the first arising from differences in strength, intelligence, and so forth, the second from the conventions that govern societies. It is the inequalities of the latter sort that he sets out to explain. Adopting what he thought the properly "scientific" method of investigating origins, he attempts to reconstruct the earliest phases of humanity's experience of life on earth. He suggests that original humans were not social beings but entirely solitary, and to this extent he agrees with Hobbes's account of the state of nature. But in contrast to the English pessimist's view of human life in such a condition, Rousseau claims that original humans, while admittedly solitary, were healthy, happy, good, and free. Human vices, he argues, date from the time when societies were formed.

Rousseau thus exonerates nature and blames society for the emergence of vices. He says that passions that generate vices hardly exist in the state of nature but begin to develop as soon as humans form societies. Rousseau goes on to suggest that societies started when people built their first huts, a development that facilitated cohabitation of males and females, which in turn produced the habit of living as a family and associating with neighbours. This "nascent society," as Rousseau calls it, was good while it lasted. Indeed, it was the "golden age" of human history. Only it did not endure. With the tender passion of love there was also born the destructive passion of jealousy. Neighbours started to compare their abilities and achievements with one another, and this "marked the first step towards inequality and at the same time towards vice." People started to demand consideration and respect, and their innocent self-love turned into culpable pride, as each person wanted to be better than everyone else.

The introduction of property marked a further step toward inequality because it necessitated instituting law and government to protect property. Rousseau laments the "fatal" concept of property in one of his more eloquent passages, describing the "horrors" that have resulted from the departure from a condition in which the earth belonged to no one. These passages in his second *Discourse* excited later revolutionaries such as Marx and Vladimir Ilich Lenin (1870–1924), but Rousseau himself did not think that the past could be undone in any way. There was no point in men dreaming of a return to the golden age.

Civil society, as Rousseau describes it, comes into being to serve two purposes: to provide peace for everyone and to ensure the right to property for anyone lucky enough to have possessions. It is thus of some advantage to everyone, but mostly to the advantage of the rich, because it transforms their de facto ownership into rightful ownership and keeps the poor dispossessed. It is a somewhat fraudulent social contract that introduces government, because the poor get so much less out of it than do the rich. Even so, the rich are no happier in civil society than are the poor because the social individual is never satisfied. Society leads people to hate one another to the extent that their interests conflict, and the best they are able to do is to hide their hostility behind a mask of courtesy. Thus Rousseau regards the inequality not as a separate problem but as one of the features of the long process by which people become alienated from nature and from innocence.

In the dedication Rousseau wrote for the *Discourse*, to present it to the republic of Geneva, he nevertheless praises that city-state for having achieved the ideal balance between "the equality which nature established among men and the inequality which they have instituted among themselves." The arrangement he discerned in Geneva was one in which the best persons were chosen by the citizens and put in the highest positions of authority. Like Plato (*c.* 428–*c.* 348 BCE), Rousseau always believed that a just society was one in which everyone was in his right place. And having written the *Discourse* to explain how human liberty had been lost in the past, he went on to write another book, *Du Contrat social* (1762; *The Social Contract*), to suggest how it might be recovered in the future. Again Geneva was the model: not Geneva as it had become in 1754, when Rousseau returned there to recover his rights as a citizen, but Geneva as it had once been (i.e., Geneva as the Protestant Reformer John Calvin [1509–64] had designed it).

The *Social Contract* begins with the sensational opening sentence, "Man is born free, and everywhere he is in chains." Rousseau proceeds to argue that these chains need not exist. If a civil society, or state, could be based on a genuine social contract, as opposed to the fraudulent social contract depicted in the *Discourse on the Origin of Inequality*, people would receive in exchange for their independence a better kind of freedom—namely, true political, or republican, liberty. Such liberty is to be found in obedience to a self-imposed law.

Rousseau's definition of political liberty raises an obvious problem. For while it can be readily agreed that an individual is free if he obeys only rules he prescribes for himself, this is so because an individual is a person with a single will. A society, by contrast, is a set of persons with a set of individual wills, and conflict between separate wills is a fact of universal experience. Rousseau's response to the problem is to define his civil society as an artificial person united by a general will, or *volonté générale*. The social contract that brings society into being is a pledge, and the society remains in being as a pledged group. Rousseau's republic is a creation of the general will—of a will that never falters in each and every member to further the public, common, or national interest—even though it may conflict at times with personal interest.

Rousseau sounds very much like Hobbes when he says that under the pact by which men enter civil society everyone totally alienates himself and all his rights to the whole community. Rousseau, however, represents this act as a form of exchange of rights whereby people give up natural rights in return for civil rights. The bargain is a good one, because what is surrendered are rights of dubious value, whose realization depends solely on an individual's own might, and what is obtained in return are rights that are both legitimate and enforced by the collective might of the community.

There is no more haunting paragraph in *The Social Contract* than that in which Rousseau speaks of "forcing a man to be free." But it would be wrong to interpret these words in the manner of those critics who see Rousseau as a prophet of modern totalitarianism. He does not claim that a whole society can be forced to be free but only that an occasional individual, who is enslaved by his passions to the extent of disobeying the law, can be restored by force to obedience to the voice of the general will that exists inside of him. The person who is coerced by society for a breach of the law is, in Rousseau's view, being brought back to an awareness of his own true interests.

For Rousseau there is a radical dichotomy between true law and actual law. Actual law, which he describes in the *Discourse on the Origin of Inequality*, simply protects the status quo. True law, as described in *The Social Contract*, is just law, and what ensures its being just is that it is made by the people in its collective capacity as sovereign and obeyed by the same people in their individual capacities as subjects. Rousseau is confident that such laws could not be unjust because it is inconceivable that any people would make unjust laws for itself.

Rousseau is, however, troubled by the fact that the majority of a people does not necessarily represent its most intelligent citizens. Indeed, he agrees with Plato that most people are stupid. Thus the general will, while always morally sound, is sometimes mistaken. Hence Rousseau suggests the people need a lawgiver—a great mind like Solon (*c.* 630–*c.* 560 BCE), Lycurgus (*c.* 390–*c.* 324 BCE), or Calvin—to draw up a constitution and system of laws. He even suggests that such lawgivers need to claim divine inspiration in order to persuade the dim-witted multitude to accept and endorse the laws it is offered.

This suggestion echoes a similar proposal by Niccolò Machiavelli (1469–1527), a political theorist Rousseau greatly admired and whose love of republican government he shared. An even more conspicuously Machiavellian influence can be discerned in Rousseau's chapter on civil religion, where he argues that Christianity, despite its truth, is useless as a republican religion on the grounds that it is directed to the unseen world and does nothing to teach citizens the virtues that are needed in the service of the state—namely, courage, virility, and patriotism. Rousseau does not go so far as Machiavelli in proposing a revival of pagan cults, but he does propose a civil religion with minimal theological content designed to fortify and not impede (as Christianity impedes) the cultivation of martial virtues. It is understandable that the authorities of Geneva, profoundly convinced that the national church of their little republic was at the same time a truly Christian church and a nursery of patriotism, reacted angrily against this chapter in Rousseau's *Social Contract*.

JOHN RAWLS

The publication of *A Theory of Justice* (1971), by the American philosopher John Rawls, spurred a revival of interest in the philosophical foundations of liberalism—a political doctrine, originating with Locke, that emphasizes the rights and freedoms of the individual. According to classical liberals, the central challenge of politics is to devise a system that gives government the power necessary to protect individual liberty but also prevents those who govern from abusing that power. Modern liberals, in contrast, see a greater challenge in removing obstacles that prevent individuals from living freely or from fully realizing their potential. Such obstacles, as they conceive them, include poverty, disease, discrimination, and ignorance. Because of Rawls's work, the viability of liberalism has been a major theme of political philosophy in English-speaking countries.

In *A Theory of Justice*, Rawls observed that a necessary condition of justice in any society is that each individual should be the equal bearer of certain rights that cannot be disregarded under any circumstances, even if doing so would advance the general welfare or satisfy the demands of a majority. This condition cannot be met by utilitarianism,

John Rawls. Harvard University news office

because that ethical theory would countenance forms of government in which the greater happiness of a majority is achieved by neglecting the rights and interests of a minority. Hence, utilitarianism is unsatisfactory as a theory of justice, and another theory must be sought.

According to Rawls, a just society is one whose major political, social, and economic institutions, taken together, satisfy the following two principles:

1. Each person has an equal claim to a scheme of basic rights and liberties that is the maximum consistent with the same scheme for all.
2. Social and economic inequalities are permissible only if: (a) they confer the greatest benefit

to the least-advantaged members of society, and (b) they are attached to positions and offices open to all under conditions of fair equality of opportunity.

The basic rights and liberties in principle 1 include the rights and liberties of democratic citizenship, such as the right to vote; the right to run for office in free elections; freedom of speech, assembly, and religion; the right to a fair trial; and, more generally, the right to the rule of law. Principle 1 is accorded strict priority over principle 2, which regulates social and economic inequalities.

Principle 2 combines two ideals. The first, known as the "difference principle," requires that any unequal distribution of social or economic goods (e.g., wealth) must be such that the least-advantaged members of society would be better off under that distribution than they would be under any other distribution consistent with principle 1, including an equal distribution. (A slightly unequal distribution might benefit the least advantaged by encouraging greater overall productivity.) The second ideal is meritocracy, understood in a very demanding way. According to Rawls, fair equality of opportunity obtains in a society when all persons with the same native talent (genetic inheritance) and the same degree of ambition have the same prospects for success in all competitions for positions that confer special economic and social advantages.

But why should one suppose with Rawls that justice requires an approximately egalitarian redistribution of social and economic goods? After all, a person who prospers in a market economy might plausibly say, "I earned my wealth. Therefore, I am entitled to keep it." But how one fares in a market economy depends on luck as well as effort. There is the luck of being in the right place at the right time and of benefiting from unpredictable shifts in supply and demand, but there is also the luck of being born with greater or lesser intelligence and other desirable traits, along with the luck of growing up in a nurturing environment. No one can take credit for this kind of luck, but it decisively influences how one fares in the many competitions by which social and economic goods are distributed. Indeed, sheer brute luck is so thoroughly intermixed with the contributions one makes to one's own success (or failure) that it is ultimately impossible to distinguish what a person is responsible for from what he is not. Given this fact, Rawls urged, the only plausible justification of inequality is that it serves to render everyone better off, especially those who have the least.

Rawls tried to accommodate his theory of justice to what he takes to be the important fact that reasonable people disagree deeply about the nature of morality and the good life and will continue to do so in any nontyrannical society that respects freedom of speech. He aimed to render his theory noncommittal on these controversial matters and to posit a set of principles of justice that all reasonable persons can accept as valid, despite their disagreements. In a later work, *Political Liberalism* (1993), Rawls revised the argument for the two principles of justice by construing the contracting individuals as representatives of conflicting comprehensive worldviews in a pluralistic democracy. Rawls also wrote works on international justice and human rights and on the history of moral and political philosophy.

DEONTOLOGY

Deontological ethical theories place special emphasis on moral rules and on the related concept of duty. In deontological ethics an action is considered morally good because it conforms to a moral law, principle, or rule, not because the product of the action is good. Deontological ethics holds that at least some acts are morally obligatory (i.e., one has a duty to perform such acts, regardless of their consequences for human welfare). Descriptive of such ethics are such expressions as "Duty for duty's sake," "Virtue is its own reward," and "Let justice be done though the heavens fall." As noted in Chapter 1, deontology is typically contrasted with consequentialist (or teleological) ethics, which holds that the basic standard of morality is precisely the value of what an action brings into being.

The first great philosopher to define deontological principles was Immanuel Kant (1724–1804), the German founder of critical philosophy, whose ethics were much influenced by Christianity as well as by the Enlightenment. Kant held that nothing is absolutely good, or good without qualification, except a good will—a good will being one that wills to act in accord with the moral law and out of respect for that law, rather than out of natural inclinations. Kant saw the moral law as a categorical imperative (i.e., an unconditional command) and believed that its content could be established by human reason alone. Reason begins with the principle "Act only on that maxim whereby thou canst at the same time will that it should become a universal law." Kant's critics, however, questioned his view that all duties can be derived from this purely formal principle and have argued that, in his preoccupation with rational consistency, he neglected the concrete content of moral obligation.

This objection was addressed in the 20th century by the Scottish philosopher Sir David Ross (1877–1971), who held that numerous "prima facie duties," rather than a single formal principle for deriving them, are themselves immediately self-evident. Ross distinguished these prima facie duties (such as promise keeping, reparation, gratitude, and justice) from actual duties, for "any possible act has many sides to it which are relevant to its rightness or wrongness." These facets have to be weighed before "forming a judgment on the totality of its nature" as an actual obligation in the given circumstances.

THE ETHICS OF IMMANUEL KANT

The standard source book for the ethical doctrines of Immanuel Kant is the *Kritik der praktischen Vernunft* (1788, spelled "Critik" and "practischen"; *Critique of Practical Reason*). The earlier *Grundlegung zur Metaphysik der Sitten* (1785; *Groundwork of the Metaphysics of Morals*) is a shorter and, despite its title, more readily comprehensible treatment of the same general topic. Both differ from *Die Metaphysik der Sitten* (1797; *The Metaphysics of Morals*) in that they deal with pure ethics and try to elucidate basic principles; whereas the later work is concerned with applying what they establish in the concrete, a process that involved the consideration of virtues and vices and the foundations of law and politics.

There are many points of similarity between Kant's ethics and his epistemology, or theory of knowledge, outlined in the *Critik der reinen Vernunft* (1781, 1787; *Critique of Pure Reason*). He used the same scaffolding for both—a "Doctrine of Elements," including an "Analytic" and a "Dialectic," followed by a "Methodology," but the second *Critique* is far shorter and much less complicated. Just as the distinction between sense perception and intelligence was fundamental for the former, so is that between the inclinations and moral reason for the latter. And just as the nature of the human cognitive situation was elucidated in the first *Critique* by reference to the hypothetical notion of an intuitive understanding, so is that of the human moral situation clarified by reference to the notion of a "holy will." For a will of this kind there would be no distinction between reason and inclination. A being possessed of a holy will would always act as it ought. It would not, however, have the concepts of duty and moral obligation, which enter only when reason and desire find themselves opposed. In the case of human beings, the opposition is continuous, for humans are at the same time both flesh and spirit. Here the influence of Kant's religious background is most prominent. Hence, the moral life is a continuing struggle in which morality appears to the potential delinquent in the form of a law that demands to be obeyed for its own sake—a law, however, the commands of which are not issued by some alien authority but represent the voice of reason, which the moral subject can recognize as his own.

In the "Dialectic," Kant took up again the ideas of God, freedom, and immortality. Dismissed in the first *Critique* as objects that humans can never know because they transcend sense experience, he now argued that they are essential postulates for the moral life. Though not reachable in metaphysics, they are absolutely essential for moral philosophy.

Kant is often described as an ethical rationalist, and the description is not wholly inappropriate. He never espoused, however, the radical rationalism of some of his contemporaries, including those who held that reason provides direct insight into a world of moral values or intuitive apprehension of the rightness of this or that moral principle. Thus, practical, like theoretical, reason was for Kant formal rather than material—a framework of formative principles rather than a content of actual rules. This is why he put such stress on his first formulation of the categorical imperative: "Act only on that maxim through which you can at the same time will that it should become a universal law." Lacking any insight into the moral realm, humans can only ask themselves whether what they are proposing to do has the formal character of law—the character, namely, of being the same for all persons similarly circumstanced.

NATURAL-RIGHTS THEORY

Another important variety of deontological ethics is natural-rights theory. Although the social-contract theories of Hobbes and Locke both presupposed and justified the existence of some natural rights, some later political philosophers took the notion of natural rights as absolute and defined the scope and limits of government power on the basis of this assumption. The leading 20th-century representative of this line of thinking, the American philosopher Robert Nozick (1938–2002), held that the state should have no more than minimal powers—essentially the powers to protect citizens' rights to life and property—because only a state with those powers could have come about without violating anyone's natural rights.

THE HISTORY OF NATURAL RIGHTS

The notion of natural rights has a long history, extending to ancient Greece and Rome and particularly to the Stoics. Since the end of World War II, however, what philosophers call "natural rights" have usually been referred to outside philosophical circles as "human rights." This is partly because the concept of natural law, to which the concept of natural rights was intimately linked, was philosophically murky and had become a matter of great controversy in secular political debates.

Origins in Ancient Greece and Rome

The Stoics held that human conduct should be judged according to, and brought into harmony with, the law of nature. A classic example of this view is given in the play *Antigone*, by Sophocles (c. 496–406 BCE), in which the title character, upon being reproached by King Creon for defying his command not to bury her slain brother, asserted that she acted in accordance with the immutable laws of the gods.

In part because Stoicism played a key role in its formation and spread, Roman law similarly allowed for the existence of a natural law and with it—pursuant to the *jus gentium* ("law of nations")—certain universal rights that extended beyond the rights of citizenship. According to the Roman jurist Ulpian (died 228 CE), for example, natural law was that which nature, not the state, assures to all human beings, Roman citizens or not.

It was not until after the Middle Ages, however, that natural law became explicitly associated with natural rights. In Greco-Roman and medieval times, doctrines of natural law concerned mainly the duties, rather than the

Stoic thought is exemplified in Sophocles's play Antigone, *when Antigone, chastised by King Creon for burying her brother, claims she acted in accordance with the laws of the gods.* Anne-Christine Poujoulat/AFP/ Getty Images

rights, of "Man." Moreover, as evidenced in the writings of Aristotle (384–322 BCE) and St. Thomas Aquinas (c. 1224–1274), these doctrines recognized the legitimacy of slavery and serfdom and, in so doing, excluded perhaps the most important ideas of natural or human rights as they are understood today—freedom (or liberty) and equality.

For the idea of natural rights to gain general recognition, therefore, certain basic societal changes were necessary, changes of the sort that took place gradually, beginning with the decline of European feudalism from about the 13th century and continuing through the Renaissance to the Peace of Westphalia (1648). During this period, resistance to religious intolerance and political and economic bondage; the evident failure of rulers to meet their obligations under natural law; and the unprecedented commitment to individual expression and worldly experience that was characteristic of the Renaissance all combined to shift the conception of natural law from *duties* to *rights*. The teachings of Aquinas and Hugo Grotius (1583–1645) on the European continent, and the Magna Carta (1215), the Petition of Right of 1628, and the English Bill of Rights (1689) in England, were proof of this change. Each testified to the increasingly popular view that human beings are endowed with certain eternal and inalienable rights that never were renounced when humankind "contracted" to enter the social from the primitive state and never diminished by the claim of the "divine right of kings."

Divine Right of Kings

The divine right of kings was a political and religious doctrine designed to justify monarchical absolutism. It asserted that kings derived their authority from God and could not therefore be held accountable for their actions by any earthly authority such as a parliament. Originating in Europe, the divine-right theory can be traced to the medieval conception of God's award of temporal power to the political ruler, paralleling the award of spiritual power to the church. By the 16th and 17th centuries, however, the new national monarchs were asserting their authority in matters of both church and state. King James I of England (reigned 1603–25) was the foremost exponent of the divine right of kings, but the doctrine virtually disappeared from English politics after the Glorious Revolution (1688–89). In the late 17th and the 18th centuries, kings such as Louis XIV (1643–1715) of France continued to profit from the divine-right theory, even though many of them no longer had any truly religious belief in it. The American Revolution (1775–83), the French Revolution (1789), and the Napoleonic wars deprived the doctrine of most of its remaining credibility.

The bishop Jacques-Bénigne Bossuet (1627–1704), one of the principal French theorists of divine right, asserted that the king's person and authority were sacred; his power was modeled on that of a father's and was absolute, deriving from God; and he was governed by reason (i.e., custom and precedent). In the middle of the 17th century, the English Royalist squire Sir Robert Filmer (1588–1653) likewise held that the state was a family and that the king was a father, but he claimed, in an interpretation of Scripture, that Adam was the first king and that Charles I (reigned 1625–49) ruled England as Adam's eldest heir. The antiabsolutist philosopher John Locke (1632–1704) wrote his *First Treatise of Civil Government* (1689) in order to refute such arguments.

The doctrine of divine right can be dangerous for both church and state. For the state it suggests that secular authority is conferred, and can therefore be removed, by the church, and for the church it implies that kings have a direct relationship to God and may therefore dictate to ecclesiastical rulers.

Natural Law Transformed into Natural Rights

The modern conception of natural law as meaning or implying natural rights was elaborated primarily by thinkers of the 17th and 18th centuries. The intellectual and the scientific achievements of the 17th century—including the materialism of Thomas Hobbes, the rationalism of René Descartes (1596–1650) and

Gottfried Wilhelm Leibniz (1646–1716), the pantheism of Benedict de Spinoza (1632–77), and the empiricism of Francis Bacon (1561–1626) and John Locke—encouraged a belief in natural law and universal order. During the 18th century, the so-called Age of Enlightenment, a growing confidence in human reason and in the perfectibility of human affairs led to the more comprehensive expression of this belief. Particularly important were the writings of Locke, arguably the most important natural-law theorist of modern times, and the works of the 18th-century philosophes centred mainly in Paris, including Montesquieu (1689–1755), Voltaire (1694–1778), and Jean-Jacques Rousseau (1712–78). Locke argued in detail, mainly in writings associated with the English Glorious Revolution, that certain rights self-evidently pertain to individuals as human beings (because these rights existed in "the state of nature" before humankind entered civil society); that chief among them are the rights to life, liberty (freedom from arbitrary rule), and property; that, upon entering civil society, humankind surrendered to the state—pursuant to a social contract—only the right to enforce these natural rights and not the rights themselves; and that the state's failure to secure these rights gives rise to a right to responsible, popular revolution. The philosophes, building on Locke and others and embracing many and varied currents of thought with a common supreme faith in reason, vigorously attacked religious and scientific dogmatism, intolerance, censorship, and social and economic restraints. They sought to discover and act upon universally valid principles governing nature, humanity, and society, including the inalienable "rights of Man," which they treated as a fundamental ethical and social gospel.

Not surprisingly, this liberal intellectual ferment exerted a profound influence in the Western world of the late 18th and early 19th centuries. Together with the Glorious Revolution in England and the resulting English Bill of Rights, it provided the rationale for the wave of revolutionary agitation that swept the West, most notably in North America and France. Thomas Jefferson (1743–1826), who had studied Locke and Montesquieu, gave poetic eloquence to the plain prose of the 17th century in the Declaration of Independence, proclaimed by the 13 American colonies on July 4, 1776: "We hold these truths to be self-evident, that all men are created equal, that they are endowed by their Creator with certain unalienable Rights, that among these are Life, Liberty and the Pursuit of Happiness." Similarly, the marquis de Lafayette (1757–1834), who won the close friendship of George Washington (1732–99) and who shared the hardships of the American Revolution, imitated the pronouncements of the English and American revolutions in the Declaration of the Rights of Man and of the Citizen of Aug. 26, 1789, proclaiming that "men are born and remain free and equal in rights" and that "the aim of every political association is the preservation of the natural and imprescriptible rights of man."

In sum, the idea of natural rights, though now known by another name, played a key role in late 18th- and early 19th-century struggles against political absolutism. It was, indeed, the failure of rulers to respect the principles of freedom and equality that was responsible for this development.

"Nonsense Upon Stilts": The Critics of Natural Rights

The idea of natural rights was not without its detractors, however. In the first place, because it was frequently associated with religious orthodoxy, the doctrine of natural rights became less attractive to philosophical and political liberals. Additionally, because they were conceived in essentially absolutist terms, natural rights were increasingly considered to conflict with one another. Most importantly, the doctrine of natural rights came under powerful philosophical and political attack from both the right and the left.

In England, for example, conservative political thinkers such as Edmund Burke (1729–97) and David Hume (1711–76) united with liberals such as Jeremy Bentham (1748–1832) to condemn the doctrine, the former out of fear that public affirmation of natural rights would lead to social upheaval, the latter out of concern lest declarations and proclamations of natural rights substitute for effective legislation. In his *Reflections on the Revolution in France* (1790), Burke—a believer in natural law who nonetheless denied that the "rights of Man" could be derived from it—criticized the drafters of the Declaration of the Rights of Man and of the Citizen for proclaiming the "monstrous fiction" of human equality, which, he argued, serves but to inspire "false ideas and vain expectations in men destined to travel in the obscure walk of laborious life." Bentham, one of the founders of utilitarianism, was no less scornful. "Rights," he wrote, "is the child of law; from real law come real rights; but from imaginary laws, from 'law of nature,' come imaginary rights....Natural rights is simple nonsense; natural and imprescriptible rights (an American phrase)...[is] rhetorical nonsense, nonsense upon stilts." Agreeing with Bentham, Hume insisted that natural law and natural rights are unreal metaphysical phenomena.

This assault upon natural law and natural rights intensified and broadened during the 19th and early 20th centuries. John Stuart Mill, despite his vigorous defense of liberty, proclaimed that rights ultimately are founded on utility. The German jurist Friedrich Karl von Savigny (1779–1861), England's Sir Henry Maine (1822–88), and other "historicalist" legal thinkers emphasized that rights are a function of cultural and environmental variables unique to particular communities. The English jurist John Austin (1790–1859) argued that the only law is "the command of the sovereign" (a phrase of Hobbes). And the logical positivists of the early 20th century insisted that the only truth is that which can be established by verifiable experience and that therefore ethical pronouncements (along with religious and metaphysical pronouncements) are not cognitively significant. By World War I, there were scarcely any theorists who would defend the "rights of Man" along the lines of natural law. Indeed, under the influence of 19th-century German Idealism and parallel expressions of rising European nationalism, there were some—the Marxists, for example—who, though not rejecting individual rights altogether, maintained that rights, from whatever source derived, belong to communities or whole societies and nations preeminently.

The Persistence of the Notion

Although the heyday of natural rights proved short, the idea of rights nonetheless endured. The abolition of slavery, the implementation of factory legislation, the rise of popular education and trade unionism, the universal suffrage movement—these and other examples of 19th-century reformist impulses afford ample evidence that the idea was not to be extinguished, even if its ultimate justification had become a matter of general skepticism. But it was not until the rise and fall of Nazi Germany that the idea of natural rights, by then referred to as human rights, truly came into its own. Many of the gruesome atrocities committed by the Nazi regime had been officially authorized by Nazi laws and decrees, and this fact convinced many that law and morality cannot be grounded in any purely utilitarian or other consequentialist doctrine. Certain actions, according to this view, are absolutely wrong, no matter what the circumstances; human beings are entitled to simple respect, at least.

Today the vast majority of legal scholars and philosophers—particularly in the liberal West—agree that every human being has, at least in theory, some basic rights. Indeed, the last half of the 20th century may fairly be said to mark the birth of the international as well as the universal recognition of human rights. In the charter establishing the United Nations, for example, all member states

When Nazi laws and decrees sanctioned the regime's atrocious crimes, many were persuaded that some actions are unconditionally wrong, regardless of the circumstances. FPG/Archive Photos/Getty Images

pledged themselves to take joint and separate action for the achievement of "universal respect for, and observance of, human rights and fundamental freedoms for all without distinction as to race, sex, language, or religion." In the Universal Declaration of Human Rights, representatives from many cultures endorsed the rights therein set forth "as a common standard of achievement for all peoples and all nations." And in 1976 the International Covenant on Economic, Social and Cultural Rights and the International Covenant on Civil and Political Rights, each approved by the UN General Assembly in 1966, entered into force and effect.

ROBERT NOZICK

In the 20th century the most influential philosophical defender of natural rights was Robert Nozick. The political philosophy he adhered to, libertarianism, is essentially a classical form of liberalism that holds that any government power beyond the minimum necessary to protect life and property is unjustified. Ironically, given his subsequent political philosophy, Nozick was a member of the student New Left and an enthusiastic socialist during his high school and college years. At Columbia University in New York City he helped to found a campus branch of the League for Industrial Democracy, a precursor of the leftist Students for a Democratic Society. While in graduate school, however, he read works by libertarian economists such as F.A. Hayek and Ludwig von Mises, and his political views began to change. His conversion to libertarianism culminated in 1974 with the publication of *Anarchy, State, and Utopia*, a closely argued and highly original defense of the libertarian "minimal state" and a critique of the social-democratic liberalism of his Harvard colleague John Rawls. Immediately hailed by

Prominent libertarian philosopher Robert Nozick was the most influential philosophical advocate for natural rights in the 20th century. Martha Holmes/Time & Life Pictures/Getty Images

conservative intellectuals, the work became a kind of philosophical manifesto of the American New Right, though Nozick himself was not entirely comfortable with this association.

Libertarianism

Libertarianism is a political philosophy that takes individual liberty to be the primary political value. It may be understood as a form of liberalism, the political philosophy associated with the English philosophers John Locke and John Stuart Mill, the Scottish economist Adam Smith, and the American statesman Thomas Jefferson. Liberalism seeks to define and justify the legitimate powers of government in terms of certain natural or God-given individual rights. These rights include the rights to life, liberty, private property, freedom of speech and association, freedom of worship, government by consent, equality under the law, and moral autonomy (the pursuit of one's own conception of happiness, or the "good life"). The purpose of government, according to liberals, is to protect these and other individual rights, and in general liberals have contended that government power should be limited to that which is necessary to accomplish this task. Libertarians are classical liberals who strongly emphasize the individual right to liberty. They contend that the scope and powers of government should be constrained so as to allow each individual as much freedom of action as is consistent with a like freedom for everyone else. Thus, they believe that individuals should be free to behave and to dispose of their property as they see fit, provided that their actions do not infringe on the equal freedom of others.

Justification of the Minimal State

The main purpose of *Anarchy, State, and Utopia* is to show that the minimal state, and only the minimal state, is morally justified. By a minimal state Nozick means a state that functions essentially as a "night watchman," with powers limited to those necessary to protect citizens against violence, theft, and fraud. By arguing that the minimal state is justified, Nozick seeks to refute anarchism, which opposes any state whatsoever. By arguing that no more than the minimal state is justified, Nozick seeks to refute modern forms of liberalism, as well as socialism and other leftist ideologies, which contend that, in addition to its powers as a night watchman, the state should have the powers to regulate the economic activities of citizens, to redistribute wealth in the direction of greater equality, and to provide social services such as education and health care.

Against anarchism, Nozick claims that a minimal state is justified because it (or something quite like it) would arise spontaneously among people living in a hypothetical "state of nature" through transactions that would not involve the violation of anyone's natural rights. Following Locke, Nozick assumes that everyone possesses the natural rights to life, liberty, and property, including the right to claim as property the fruits or products of one's labour and the right to dispose of one's property as one sees fit (provided that in doing so one does not violate the rights of anyone else). Everyone also has the natural right to punish those who violate or attempt to violate one's own natural rights. Because defending one's natural rights in a state of nature would be difficult for anyone to do on his own, individuals would band together to form "protection associations," in which members would work together to defend each other's rights and to punish rights violators. Eventually, some of these associations would develop into private businesses offering protection and punishment services for a fee. The great importance that individuals would attach to such services would give the largest protection firms a natural competitive advantage, and eventually only one firm, or a confederation of firms, would control all the protection and punishment business in the community. Because this firm (or confederation of firms) would have a monopoly of force in the territory of the community and because it would protect the rights of everyone living there, it would constitute a minimal state in the libertarian sense. And because the minimal state would come about without violating anyone's natural rights, a state with at least its powers is justified.

Against liberalism and ideologies farther left, Nozick claims that no more than the minimal state is justified, because any state with more extensive powers would violate the natural rights of its citizens. Thus the state should not have the power to control prices or to set a minimum wage, because doing so would violate the natural right of citizens to dispose of their property, including their labour, as they see fit. For similar reasons, the state should not have the power to establish public education or health care through taxes imposed on citizens who may wish to spend their money on private services instead. Indeed, according to Nozick, any mandatory taxation used to fund services or benefits other than those constitutive of the minimal state is unjust, because such taxation amounts to a kind of "forced labour" for the state by those who must pay the tax.

The Entitlement Theory of Justice

Nozick's vision of legitimate state power thus contrasts markedly with that of Rawls and his followers. Rawls argues that the state should have whatever powers are necessary to ensure that those citizens who are least well-off are as well-off as they can be (though these powers must be consistent with a variety of basic rights and freedoms). This viewpoint is derived from Rawls's theory of justice, one principle of which is that an unequal distribution of wealth and income is acceptable only if those at the bottom are better off than they would be under any other distribution. Nozick's response to such arguments is to claim that they rest on a false conception of distributive justice: they wrongly define a just distribution in terms of the pattern it exhibits at a given time (e.g., an equal distribution or a distribution that is unequal to a certain extent) or in terms of the historical circumstances surrounding its development (e.g., those who worked the hardest have more) rather than in terms of the nature of the transactions through which the distribution came about. For Nozick, any distribution of "holdings," as he calls them, no matter how unequal, is just if (and only if) it arises from a just distribution through legitimate means. One legitimate means is the appropriation of something that is unowned in circumstances where the acquisition would not disadvantage others. A second means is the voluntary transfer of ownership of holdings to someone else. A third means is the rectification of past injustices in the acquisition or transfer of holdings. According to Nozick, anyone who acquired what he has through these means is morally entitled to it. Thus the "entitlement" theory of justice states that the distribution of holdings in a society is just if (and only if) everyone in that society is entitled to what he has.

To show that theories of justice based on patterns or historical circumstances are false, Nozick devised a simple but ingenious objection, which came to be known as the "Wilt Chamberlain" argument. Assume, he says, that the distribution of holdings in a given society is just according to some theory based on patterns or historical circumstances—e.g., the egalitarian theory, according to which only a strictly equal distribution of holdings is just. In this society, Wilt Chamberlain is an excellent basketball player, and many teams compete with each other to engage his services. Chamberlain eventually agrees to play for a certain team on the condition that everyone who attends a game in which he plays puts 25 cents in a

Robert Nozick used his "Wilt Chamberlain" argument to refute theories of justice based on patterns or historical circumstances. George Long/WireImage/Getty Images

special box at the gate, the contents of which will go to him. During the season, one million fans attend the team's games, and so Chamberlain receives $250,000. Now, however, the supposedly just distribution of holdings is upset, because Chamberlain has $250,000 more than anyone else. Is the new distribution unjust? The strong intuition that it is not unjust is accounted for by Nozick's entitlement theory (because Chamberlain acquired his holdings by legitimate means) but conflicts with the egalitarian theory. Nozick contends that this argument generalizes to any theory based on patterns or historical circumstances, because any distribution dictated by such a theory could be upset by ordinary and unobjectionable transactions like the one involving Chamberlain. Nozick concludes that any society that attempted to implement such a theory would have to intrude grossly on the liberty of its citizens in order to enforce the distribution it considers just. "The socialist society," as he puts it, "would have to forbid capitalist acts between consenting adults."

Nozick emphasizes that his vision of the minimal state is inclusive and is compatible with the existence of smaller communities based on varying theories of justice. A group that wished to form a socialist community governed by an egalitarian theory would be free to do so, as long as it did not force others to join the community against their will. Indeed, every group would enjoy the same freedom to realize its own idea of a good society. In this way, according to Nozick, the minimal state constitutes a "framework for utopia."

Anarchy, State, and Utopia has generated an enormous secondary literature, much of it critical. Unlike Rawls, however, Nozick did not attempt to defend or revise his political views in published work. Nozick's other books include *Philosophical Explanations* (1981), *The Nature of Rationality* (1993), and *Invariances: The Structure of the Objective World* (2001).

FEMINISM

Feminist ethics is one aspect of a much broader movement known as philosophical feminism. Feminism in this sense is a loosely related set of approaches in various fields of philosophy that emphasizes the role of gender (one's identity as "male" or "female") in the formation of traditional philosophical problems and concepts. Feminist philosophers analyze the ways in which traditional philosophy reflects and perpetuates bias against women, and they defend philosophical concepts and theories that presume women's equality with men.

THE NATURE AND SCOPE OF PHILOSOPHICAL FEMINISM

Philosophical feminism arose during the women's movement of the 1960s and '70s. During that period women in many academic disciplines, including philosophy, began to question why there were almost no works by women in the canons of their disciplines and why there were so few women in their professions. For feminist philosophers, part of the answer lay in the generally disparaging view of women that pervaded Western culture and was consequently reflected in the thinking of most male philosophers: compared with men, women were seen as irrational, emotional, unintelligent, and morally immature. Eventually, women philosophers were led to ask more pointed questions: how has philosophy been affected by the larger culture's attitudes toward women? What has philosophy left out or misunderstood because of those attitudes? The most obvious results, as women philosophers noted, were omissions. Until the late 20th century, women's philosophical contributions were generally dismissed (if they were noticed at all), and issues of concern to women were ignored. In the history of Western philosophy up to the 1970s, the topic of gender seldom arose, and when it did it was usually in the context of a rationalization of women's lower social status and their exclusion from public life. The exceptions to this rule, such as Plato's *Republic* and John Stuart Mill's *The Subjection of Women* (1861), were few and far between.

Feminist philosophers soon came to realize, however, that the problem they had identified could not be solved by filling in a few gaps (e.g., by hiring more women philosophers and by recognizing more philosophical works by women). Because of the historical sexism of Western culture and because the paradigmatic philosopher was conceived of as highly rational, dispassionate, and independent, the female philosopher was virtually a contradiction in terms. A woman could be a philosopher only if she "thought like a man." Gender bias was thus built into the qualifications for membership in the profession.

If bias against women was not incidental to philosophy but in fact one of its defining features, the potential ramifications of a feminist critique were boundless. Although some feminist philosophers adhered to mainstream philosophical traditions and pursued women's issues within those frameworks, others were convinced that treating gender as a category of philosophical analysis would entail major modifications in the practice of philosophy. Different topics would be salient; different assumptions would make sense; different methods would be appropriate. For these philosophers, pursuing a gender-based critique of philosophy to its logical conclusion would transform the discipline and give rise to a distinctively feminist approach to philosophical problems.

There were some early attempts in the history of philosophy to address issues of concern to women, including Mill's *The Subjection of Women*, which argued for woman suffrage, and *The Second Sex* (1949), by Simone de Beauvoir (1908–86), which showed how prevailing notions of femininity served male interests. Still, feminist philosophy from the 1970s was no less indebted to the practices and positions originally developed in women's consciousness-raising groups (groups dedicated to raising awareness of women's issues).

Feminist Ethics

Feminist ethics was initially developed by women who were or had been full-time homemakers or mothers and who felt excluded (and in some cases offended) by the women's movement's emphasis on dismantling barriers to professional careers for women. These women's moral worlds were less concerned with rights and justice and instead revolved around caregiving and maintaining networks of relationships. Inspired by Carol Gilligan's work on care ethics, early projects in feminist ethics shifted the focus of ethics from relations between citizens or strangers to close relationships rooted in emotional attachments, including friends, lovers, and mothers and children. In those intimate relationships, the parties respond to each other as unique individuals, not merely as typical human beings. Although they are vulnerable to each other in many of the same ways that strangers are, they are far more vulnerable to insensitivity, indifference, unkindness, and the threat of abandonment. Moreover, personal relationships are not always reciprocal. Because one of the individuals may be temporarily or chronically dependent on the other for sustenance, the other may shoulder a greater share of the burdens of the relationship. In those contexts, then, moral reciprocity is not reducible to equal respect or equal contribution.

The focus on interpersonal morality showed that general moral rules, which some traditional ethical theories strove to develop, were rather crude instruments for conducting a moral life. Consequently, feminist ethical philosophers—notably Sara Ruddick, Virginia Held, and Annette Baier—sought to explicate virtues and values suitable to everyday sociability. They questioned the tenability of basing moral relations on an implied social contract—in which individuals promise to behave

In Le Deuxième Sexe *(The Second Sex)*, *Simone de Beauvoir revealed how male interests were served by prevailing notions of femininity.* Archive Photos/Getty Images

morally toward others on the condition they behave morally toward them—and they demonstrated the critical role of trust in establishing an environment conducive to moral interaction. Although they did not repudiate the rational calculation of consequences in evaluating actions, they saw empathy and emotional responsiveness as vital to moral judgment. That general approach came to be known as the ethics of care.

Moral Psychology

Moral psychology is the study of the development of the moral sense (i.e., the capacity for forming judgments about what is morally right or wrong, good or bad). The U.S. psychologist Lawrence Kohlberg hypothesized that people's development of moral standards passes through several levels. At the early level, that of preconventional moral reasoning, the child uses external and physical events (such as pleasure or pain) as the source for moral decisions. His standards are based strictly on what will avoid punishment or bring pleasure. At the intermediate level, that of conventional moral reasoning, the child or adolescent views moral standards as a way of maintaining the approval of authority figures, chiefly his parents, and acts in accordance with their precepts. At the third level, that of postconventional moral reasoning, the adult bases his moral standards on principles that he himself has evaluated and accepts as inherently valid, regardless of society's opinion. Beginning in the 1970s, Kohlberg's work was criticized by psychologists and philosophers influenced by feminism. According to Carol Gilligan, Kohlberg's stages are inherently sexist, because they equate moral maturity with an orientation toward moral problems that is socially instilled in males but not in females. Whereas the male "ethic of rights and justice" treats morality in terms of abstract principles and conceives of moral agents as essentially autonomous, acting independently of their social situations according to general rules, the female "ethic of care" treats morality in terms of concrete bonds to particular individuals based on feelings of care and responsibility and conceives of moral agents as connected and interdependent through their feelings of care and responsibility for each other.

Because the demands of caregiving often prevented women from pursuing other projects and goals, striking a proper balance between caring for others and caring for oneself became a key problem for feminist ethics. In work since the 1990s (e.g., by Margaret Walker), the concerns addressed by the ethics of care have been reframed in sophisticated accounts of the social processes through which individuals consolidate their moral identities, enter into and sustain relationships, and negotiate responsibilities.

FEMINIST SOCIAL AND POLITICAL PHILOSOPHY

The earliest feminist philosophers examined gender bias in traditional social and political institutions. By asking the question "Who benefits?" they showed how mostly unspoken practices of gender-based exclusion and discrimination favoured the interests of men. Much of their analysis concerned sexual and family relations, which were then considered private or personal matters that could not (or should not) be addressed by political means. Accordingly, with a fine disregard, they adopted the rallying cry "the personal is political."

Whereas the traditional political philosophies of liberalism and Marxism generally ignored sexual and family issues, feminist philosophers made them the focus of political theory. Eventually three major schools of feminist political theory arose, each emphasizing a distinctive subset of issues: liberal feminism, socialist feminism, and radical feminism.

Liberal feminists (e.g., Susan Moller Okin) pointed out the many ways in which gender discrimination defeats women's aspirations, and they defended reforms designed to make women's equality a social and political reality. Noting that differences in the ways in which girls and boys are raised served to channel women and men into different and unequal social roles, they advocated gender-neutral forms of education and child rearing. They particularly focused on protecting and extending the rights that enabled women to pursue self-chosen goals, such as reproductive rights (including the right to legally obtain an abortion) and rights to full educational and economic opportunities.

Whereas liberal feminists applied the core liberal values of freedom and equality to address women's concerns, the socialist feminists Alison Jaggar and Iris Marion Young appropriated Marxist categories, which were based on labour and economic structures. Criticizing traditional Marxism for exaggerating the importance of waged labour outside the home, socialist feminists insisted that the unpaid caregiving and homemaking that women are expected to perform are equally indispensable forms of labour and that the sexual division of labour that assigns most domestic work to women is exploitative. They also objected to the double day of work that burdens most women who have children and who work outside the home. Likewise, they condemned the economic dependency and insecurity of stay-at-home mothers and the low salaries of child-care workers.

Last, the school of radical feminism turned women's attention to sexuality and to the disparities of power that pervade heterosexual relationships in patriarchal cultures. One interesting account of sexual equality and the obstacles to attaining it emerged in the work of the American feminist legal theorist Catharine A. MacKinnon. She asserted that the struggle to overcome male domination is faced with a deeply entrenched adversary: sexual desire between heterosexual women and men. The subjugation of women in society strongly influences conventional standards of femininity and masculinity, which in turn determine what heterosexual individuals find attractive in the opposite sex. Thus, according to MacKinnon, heterosexual women tend to find dominant men sexually attractive, while heterosexual men tend to find submissive women sexually attractive. The latter is the stronger and more important dynamic, since men as a group are politically, economically, and socially more powerful than women. The upshot is that the ordinary and widespread sexual attraction between heterosexual women and men is corrupted by a kind of sadism. The struggle for equal rights and equal power for women is opposed not only by laws, institutions, and practices but also by sexual desire itself. Given this analysis, the legal and cultural tolerance of pornography, which makes the subordination of women sexually appealing to men, is immoral. Pornography serves only to perpetuate a regime of sex-based domination that any decent society should reject. Such assertions provided the basis of Marilyn Frye's endorsement of separatist feminist practices.

Liberal, socialist, and radical feminism continue to challenge standard philosophical assumptions about the scope of politics and the nature of justice. Yet, arguably, each of them rests on a flawed conception of gender. As Elizabeth V. Spelman, María Lugones, and Judith Butler claimed, none adequately takes into account the ways in which gender is influenced by and interacts with sexual orientation, race, ethnicity, class, age, and ability, and none explicitly addresses how those factors affect the needs of diverse groups of women. Moreover, as Uma Narayan argued, none comes to grips with the complexities of advancing women's rights internationally or with the obstacles to coordinating feminist agendas in a globalized economy. Much current work in feminist social and political philosophy—specifically in black feminist theory, queer theory, and feminist human rights theory—takes on these urgent problems. Yet, despite advances in these fields, controversy persists between Luce Irigaray's view that gender is real and Judith Butler's contention that it is an illusion.

ETHICAL EGOISM

Ethical egoism, whose name is derived from the Latin *ego*, meaning "I," is an ethical theory holding that an action is right if and only if it promotes one's self-interest. (The word is sometimes misused for egotism, the overstressing of one's own worth.)

EGOIST DOCTRINES

Egoist doctrines are less concerned with the philosophical problem of what is the self than with the common notions of a person and his concerns. They emphasize self-perfection sought through the furthering of one's own welfare and profit—allowing, however, that sometimes one may not know where these lie and must be brought to recognize them.

Many ethical theories have an egoist bias. Ancient Greek ethics bid each person to seek his own happiness (though it should be emphasized that happiness as the Greeks conceived it entailed an appropriate concern for the interests of others). In the 17th century, Thomas Hobbes (1588–1679) and Benedict de Spinoza (1632–77) held in different ways that self-preservation is the good. Those who stress the tending of one's own conscience and moral growth are likewise egoists in this sense. In contrast with such views is an ethics that is governed more by humanity's social aspects, which stresses the importance of the community rather than that of the individual. Under this head come such theories as Stoic cosmopolitanism, utilitarianism, and 20th-century communitarianism—an alternative to liberalism and libertarianism. The distinction, however, cannot always be neatly drawn.

AYN RAND

Although few contemporary philosophers are strict ethical egoists, some economists and political thinkers have been attracted to the position. In the 20th century the foremost advocate of egoism was the Russian-born American writer Ayn Rand. In a series of commercially successful novels, Rand presented her philosophy of objectivism, which essentially reversed the traditional altruistic ethics of Judaism and Christianity.

Rand graduated from the University of Petrograd in 1924 and two years later immigrated to the United States. She initially worked as a screenwriter in Hollywood and in 1931 became a naturalized U.S. citizen. Her first novel, *We, the Living*, was published in 1936. *The Fountainhead* (1943), her first best-selling novel, depicted a highly romanticized architect-hero, a superior individual whose egoism and genius prevail over timid traditionalism and social conformism. The allegorical *Atlas Shrugged* (1957), another best-seller, combined science fiction and political message in telling of an anticollectivist strike called by the management of U.S. big industry, a company of attractive, self-made men.

The political philosophy of objectivism shaped Rand's work. A deeply conservative doctrine, it posited individual effort and ability as the sole source of all genuine achievement, thereby elevating the pursuit of self-interest to the role of first principle and scorning such notions

In her successful novels, Ayn Rand promoted radical egoism and laissez-faire capitalism. New York Times Co./Archive Photos/Getty Images

as altruism and sacrifice for the common good as liberal delusions and even vices. It further held laissez-faire capitalism to be most congenial to the exercise of talent. Rand's philosophy underlay her fiction but found more direct expression in her nonfiction, including such works as *For the New Intellectual* (1961), *The Virtue of Selfishness* (1965), *Capitalism: The Unknown Ideal* (1966), *Introduction to Objectivist Epistemology* (1967), and *Philosophy: Who Needs It?* (1982). She also promoted her objectivist philosophy in the journals *The Objectivist* (1962–71) and *The Ayn Rand Letter* (1971–76).

Rand's controversial views attracted a faithful audience of admirers and followers, many of whom first encountered her novels as teenagers. Although her work influenced generations of conservative politicians and government officials in the United States, most academic philosophers considered it shallow or confused. Rand was working on an adaptation of *Atlas Shrugged* for a television miniseries when she died.

CHAPTER 3

METAETHICS

M etaethics is the subdiscipline of ethics concerned
with determining the nature of moral concepts
and judgments. Metaethics identifies a fundamental
task of the moral philosopher, the logical analysis of
(1) moral concepts such as right and wrong, obligatory
and forbidden, and good and evil; (2) the nature and
function of moral judgments or statements; and (3)
the nature of moral reasoning. Metaethics is thus to
be contrasted with normative ethics, which explores
questions such as: "What actions are right and what
are wrong?"; "How should one live and what things
should one value?"; and "Is life worth living?"

Many philosophers hold that the fundamental
questions in ethical theory are metaethical. Some even
assert that they are the only questions appropriate for
a moral philosopher and that normative questions can
be dealt with by all people in their capacity as moralists. The position of the moral philosopher is thus
analogous to that of the philosopher of science, who
considers only the elements of scientific reasoning and
remains neutral on the question of which scientific
statements are true and which false.

Major metaethical theories include naturalism,
nonnaturalism (or intuitionism), emotivism, and
prescriptivism. Naturalists, such as Ralph Barton
Perry (1876–1957), W.T. Stace (1886–1967), Richard
B. Brandt, and Geoffrey James Warnock (1923–96),

and nonnaturalists, such as G.E. Moore (1873–1958), H.A. Prichard (1871–1947), Sir David Ross (1877–1971), and A.C. Ewing (1899–1973), agree that moral language is cognitive (i.e., that moral claims can be known to be true or false). They disagree, however, on how this knowing is to be done. Naturalists hold either that these claims can be adequately justified by reasoning from statements employing only nonmoral terms or that moral terms themselves can be defined in nonmoral (natural or factlike) terms.

Intuitionists deny both of these positions and hold that moral terms are *sui generis* that moral statements are autonomous in their logical status. According to intuitionism, such statements can be known to be true or false immediately through a kind of rational intuition. Intuitionists have differed, however, over the kinds of moral truths that are amenable to direct apprehension. For example, whereas Moore thought that it is self-evident that certain things are morally valuable, Ross thought that what is known immediately is that it is our duty to do acts of a certain type.

Emotivists, notably Sir A.J. Ayer (1910–89) and Charles Stevenson (1908–79), deny that moral utterances are cognitive, holding that they consist in emotional expressions of approval or disapproval and that the nature of moral reasoning and justification must be reinterpreted to take this essential characteristic of moral utterances into account. R.M. Hare (1919–2002) and other exponents of prescriptivism take a somewhat similar approach, arguing that moral judgments are prescriptions or prohibitions of action, rather than statements of fact about the world. In *The Language of Morals* (1952), Hare argued that it is impossible to derive any prescription from a set of descriptive sentences, but he tried nevertheless to provide a foothold for moral reasoning in the constraint that moral judgments must be "universalizable": that is, that if one judges a particular action to be wrong, one must also judge any relevantly similar action to be wrong. Universalizability is not a substantive moral principle but a logical feature of the moral terms: anyone who uses such terms as "right" and "ought" is logically committed to universalizability. A sophisticated contemporary development of emotivism and projectivism, defended by the English philosopher Simon Blackburn and others under the title "quasirealism," seeks to explain how one can properly treat ethical propositions as true or false without presupposing a special domain of nonnatural facts.

The remainder of this chapter discusses some fundamental metaethical perspectives, along with the historical and ongoing controversies that have emerged from them.

MORAL REALISM AND ANTIREALISM

According to moral realists, statements about what actions are morally required or permissible and statements about what dispositions or character traits are morally virtuous or vicious (and so on) are not mere expressions of subjective preferences but are objectively true or false depending on whether they correspond with the facts of morality—just as historical or geographic statements are true or false depending on whether they fit the historical or geographic facts. As with realism in other areas, moral realism faces challenges on two fronts.

On the metaphysical front, there is obvious scope for skepticism about whether there is, or even could be, a realm of distinctively moral facts, irreducible to and apparently inexplicable in terms of the facts of nature. On the epistemological front, it has seemed to be an insuperable obstacle to moral realism to explain how, if there really were such a realm of moral facts, human beings could possibly gain access to it. Although reason alone may seem to deliver knowledge of some kinds of nonempirical truths (e.g., of logic and mathematics), it does not seem to deliver the truths of morality, and there appears to be no other special faculty by which such truths may be detected. Talk of "moral sense" or "moral intuition," though once popular, now seems merely to rename rather than to solve the problem.

On the antirealist side, attempts to reduce moral properties to natural ones (by identifying right actions with, say, those that promote happiness) have found support, but they face difficulties of their own. Indeed, they seem particularly vulnerable to Moore's celebrated "open question" argument, which points out that, because it is always a substantive and not a tautological question whether some naturalistically specified property is

Moral realists believe that judgments about what is right or wrong and what is virtuous or vicious are objectively true or false, depending on what the "moral facts" are. Jean-Claude Winkler/Photographer's Choice/Getty Images

morally good—one can always ask, for example, "Is happiness good?"—the meanings of moral terms like "good" cannot simply be identified with the property in question. Appealing to the intrinsic "queerness" of moral properties as contrasted with natural ones, some theorists, notably the Australian-born philosopher J.L. Mackie, have denied their existence altogether, propounding an error theory of moral discourse.

Other antirealists have sought to rescue moral discourse by reinterpreting it along expressivist or projectivist lines.

ETHICAL RELATIVISM

Ethical relativism is the doctrine that there are no absolute truths in ethics and that what is morally right or wrong varies from person to person or from society to society.

ARGUMENTS FOR ETHICAL RELATIVISM

Herodotus, the Greek historian of the 5th century BCE, advanced this view when he observed that different societies have different customs and that each person thinks his own society's customs are best. But no set of social customs, Herodotus said, is really better or worse than any other. Some contemporary sociologists and cultural anthropologists have argued along similar lines that morality, because it is a social product, develops differently within different cultures. Each society develops standards that are used by people within it to distinguish acceptable from unacceptable behaviour, and every judgment of right and wrong presupposes one or another of these standards. Thus, according to these researchers, if practices such as polygamy or infanticide are considered right within a society, they are right "for that society." And

Statue of seated man said to be Herodotus; in the Louvre, Paris. © Photos.com/
Jupiterimages

if the same practices are considered wrong within a different society, those practices are wrong for that society. There is no such thing as what is "really" right, apart from these social codes, for there is no culture-neutral standard to which we can appeal to determine which society's view is correct. The different social codes are all that exist.

A second type of argument for ethical relativism is due to David Hume, who claimed that moral beliefs are based on "sentiment," or emotion, rather than on reason. This idea was developed by the 20th-century school of logical positivism and by later representatives of emotivism and prescriptivism, particularly Charles Stevenson and R.M. Hare. It follows from emotivism that right and wrong are relative to individual preferences rather than to social standards.

Ethical relativism is attractive to many philosophers and social scientists because it seems to offer the best explanation of the variability of moral belief. It also offers a plausible way of explaining how ethics fits into the world as it is described by modern science. Even if the natural world ultimately consists of nothing but value-neutral facts, say the relativists, ethics still has a foundation in human feelings and social arrangements. Finally, ethical relativism seems especially well suited to explain the virtue of tolerance. If, from an objective point of view, one's own values and the values of one's society have no special

Cultural Anthropology

Cultural anthropology is the branch of anthropology that deals with the study of culture. The discipline uses the methods, concepts, and data of archaeology, ethnography, folklore, linguistics, and related fields in its descriptions and analyses of the diverse peoples of the world. Called social anthropology in Britain, its field of research was until the mid-20th century largely restricted to the small-scale (or "primitive"), non-Western societies that first began to be identified during the age of discovery. Today the field extends to all forms of human association, from village communities to corporate cultures to urban gangs. Two key perspectives used are those of holism (understanding society as a complex, interactive whole) and cultural relativism (the appreciation of cultural phenomena within their own context). Areas of study traditionally include social structure, law, politics, religion, magic, art, and technology.

standing, then an attitude of "live and let live" toward other people's values seems appropriate.

ETHICAL RELATIVISM AND POSTMODERNISM

Beginning in the 1960s and '70s, ethical relativism was associated with postmodernism, a complex philosophical movement that questioned the idea of objectivity in many areas, including ethics. Many postmodernists regarded the very idea of objectivity as a dubious invention of the modern (i.e., post-Enlightenment) era. From the time of the Enlightenment, most philosophers and scientists believed that there is an objective, universal, and unchanging truth

David Hume, oil painting by Allan Ramsay, 1766; in the Scottish National Portrait Gallery, Edinburgh. Courtesy of the Scottish National Portrait Gallery

about everything—including science, ethics, religion, and politics—and that human reason is powerful enough to discover this truth. The eventual result of rational inquiry, therefore, was to be one science, one ethics, one religion, and one politics that would be valid for all people in all eras. According to postmodernism, however, the Enlightenment-inspired idea of objective truth, which has influenced the thinking of virtually all modern scientists and philosophers, is an illusion that has now collapsed.

This development, they contend, is due largely to the work of the German philosopher Friedrich Nietzsche (1844–1900) and his followers. Nietzsche rejected the naive faith that human beliefs simply mirror reality. Instead, each of our beliefs is grounded in a "perspective" that is neither correct nor incorrect. In ethics, accordingly, there are no moral facts but only moral interpretations of phenomena, which give rise to different existing moral codes. We may try to understand these moralities by investigating their histories and the psychology of the people who embrace them, but there is no question of proving one or another of them to be "true." Nietzsche argues, for example, that those who accept the Judeo-Christian ethical system, which he calls a "slave morality," suffer from weak and fearful personalities. A different and stronger sort of person, he says, would reject this ethic and create his own values.

Postmodernists believe that Western society has passed beyond the modern intellectual era and is now in a postmodern period characterized partly by the realization that human life and thought is a mosaic comprising many perspectives. "Truths," including the truths of science as well as ethics, should be recognized as beliefs associated with particular traditions that serve particular purposes in particular times and places. The desire for absolutes is seen as a misguided quest for the impossible. During the last half of the 20th century, the most prominent advocates of this view were Michel Foucault (1926–84) and Jacques Derrida (1930–2004).

CRITICISMS OF ETHICAL RELATIVISM

Ethical relativism, then, is a radical doctrine that is contrary to what many thoughtful people commonly assume. As such, it should not be confused with the uncontroversial thought that what is right depends on the circumstances. Everyone, absolutists and relativists alike, agrees that circumstances make a difference. Whether it is morally permissible to enter a house, for example, depends on whether one is the owner, a guest, or a burglar. Nor is ethical relativism merely the idea that different people have different beliefs about ethics, which again no one would deny. It is, rather, a theory about the status of moral beliefs, according to which none of them is objectively true. A consequence of the theory is that there is no way to justify any moral principle as valid for all people and all societies.

Critics have lodged a number of complaints against this doctrine. They point out that if ethical relativism is correct, it would mean that even the most outrageous practices, such as slavery and the physical abuse of women, are "right" if they are countenanced by the standards of the relevant society. Relativism therefore deprives us of any means of raising moral objections against horrendous social customs, provided that those customs are approved by the codes of the societies in which they exist.

But should we not be tolerant of other cultures? Critics reply that it depends on what sort of social differences are at issue. Tolerance may seem like a good policy where benign differences between cultures are concerned, but it does not seem so when, for example, a society engages in officially approved genocide, even within its own borders. And in any case, the critics say, it is a mistake to think that relativism implies that we should be tolerant, because tolerance is simply another value about which people or societies may disagree. Only an absolutist could say that tolerance is objectively good.

Moreover, the critics continue, we sometimes want to criticize our own society's values, and ethical relativism deprives us of the means of doing that as well. If ethical relativism is correct, we could not make sense of reforming or improving our own society's morals, for there would be no standard against which our society's existing practices could be judged deficient. Abandoning slavery, for example, would not be moral progress; it would only be replacing one set of standards with another.

Critics also point out that disagreement about ethics does not mean that there can be no objective truth. After all, people disagree even about scientific matters. Some people believe that disease is caused by evil spirits, while others believe it is caused by microbes, but we do not on that account conclude that disease has no "real" cause. The same might be true of ethics—disagreement might only mean that some people are more enlightened than others.

But there is actually far less disagreement than the relativists imply. Anthropologists have observed that, while there is some variation from culture to culture, there are also some values that all societies have in common. Some values are, in fact, necessary for society to exist. Without rules requiring truthfulness, for example, there could be no communication, and without rules against murder and assault, people could not live together. These are, not surprisingly, among the values that anthropologists find wherever they look. Such disagreements as do exist take place against a background of agreement on these large matters.

Lastly, to the claim that there is no legitimate way to judge a society's practices "from the outside," critics may reply that we can always ask whether a particular cultural practice works to the advantage or disadvantage of the people within the culture. If, for example, female genital

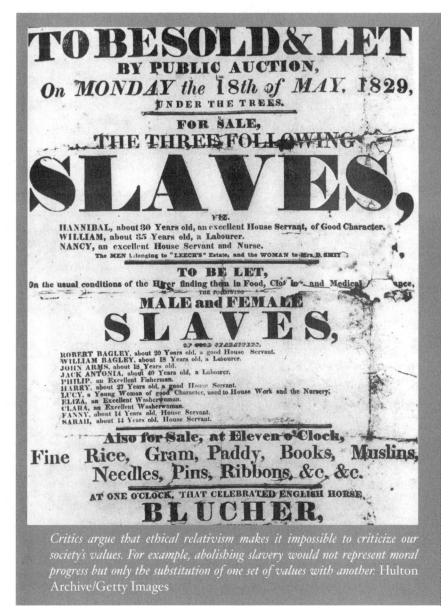

Critics argue that ethical relativism makes it impossible to criticize our society's values. For example, abolishing slavery would not represent moral progress but only the substitution of one set of values with another. Hulton Archive/Getty Images

mutilation does more harm than good for the members of the societies that practice it, that fact may be an objective reason for judging the practice to be bad. Thus the appeal to what is helpful or harmful appears to be a standard that transcends local disagreements and variations.

THE PROBLEM OF MORAL RESPONSIBILITY

The problem of moral responsibility is that of reconciling the belief that people are morally responsible for what they do with the apparent fact that humans do not have free will because their actions are causally determined. It is an ancient and enduring philosophical puzzle.

FREEDOM AND RESPONSIBILITY

Historically, most proposed solutions to the problem of moral responsibility have attempted to establish that humans do have free will. But what does free will consist of? When people make decisions or perform actions, they usually feel as though they are choosing or acting freely. A person may decide, for example, to buy apples instead of oranges, to vacation in France rather than in Italy, or to call a sister in Nebraska instead of a brother in Florida. Nevertheless, there are at least some situations in which people seem not to act freely, as when they are physically coerced or mentally or emotionally manipulated. One way to formalize the intuitive idea of free action is to say that a person acts freely if it is true that he could have acted otherwise. Buying apples is ordinarily a free action because in ordinary circumstances one can buy oranges instead. Nothing forces one to buy apples or prevents one from buying oranges.

Choosing what fruit to buy seems to be an act of free will, given that in ordinary cases nothing forces a person to buy one kind of fruit rather than another.
Keren Su/The Image Bank/Getty Images

Yet the decisions a person makes are the result of his desires, and his desires are determined by his circumstances, his past experiences, and his psychological and personality traits—his dispositions, tastes, temperament, intelligence, and so on. Circumstances, experiences, and traits in this sense are obviously the result of many factors outside the individual's control, including his upbringing and perhaps even his genetic makeup. If this is correct, a person's actions may ultimately be no more the result of free will than his eye colour.

The existence of free will seems to be presupposed by the notion of moral responsibility. Most people would agree that a person cannot be morally responsible for actions that he could not help but perform. Moreover, moral praise and blame, or reward and punishment, seem to make sense only on the assumption that the agent in question is morally responsible. These considerations seem to imply a choice between two implausible alternatives: either (1) people have free will, in which case a person's actions are not determined by his circumstances, past experiences, and psychological and personality traits, or (2) people do not have free will, in which case no one is ever morally responsible for what he does. This dilemma is the problem of moral responsibility.

DETERMINISM

Determinism is the view that, given the state of the universe (the complete physical properties of all its parts) at a certain time and the laws of nature operative in the universe at that time, the state of the universe at any subsequent time is completely determined. No subsequent state of the universe can be other than what it is. Because human actions, at an appropriate level of description, are part of the universe, it follows that humans cannot act otherwise than they do. Free will is impossible. (It is important to distinguish determinism from mere causation. Determinism is not the thesis that every event has a cause, since causes do not always necessitate their effects. It is, rather, the thesis that every event is causally inevitable. If an event has occurred, then it is impossible that it could not have occurred, given the previous state of the universe and the laws of nature.)

Philosophers and scientists who believe that the universe is deterministic and that determinism is incompatible with free will are called "hard" determinists. Because moral responsibility seems to require free will, hard determinism implies that no one is morally responsible for his actions. Although the conclusion is strongly counterintuitive, some hard determinists have insisted that the weight of philosophical argument requires that it be accepted. There is no alternative but to reform the intuitive beliefs in freedom and moral responsibility. Other hard determinists, acknowledging that such reform is scarcely feasible, hold that there may be social benefits to feeling and exhibiting moral emotions, even though the emotions themselves are based on a fiction. Such benefits are reason enough for holding fast to prephilosophical beliefs about free will and moral responsibility, according to these thinkers.

The extreme alternative to determinism is indeterminism, the view that at least some events have no deterministic cause but occur randomly, or by chance. Indeterminism is supported to some extent by research in quantum mechanics, which suggests that some events at the quantum level are in principle unpredictable (and therefore random).

LIBERTARIANISM

Philosophers and scientists who believe that the universe is indeterministic and that humans possess free will are known as "libertarians" (libertarianism in this sense is not to be confused with the school of political philosophy called libertarianism). Although it is possible to hold that the universe is indeterministic and that human actions are nevertheless determined, few contemporary philosophers defend this view.

Libertarianism is vulnerable to what is called the "intelligibility" objection. This objection points out that a person can have no more control over a purely random action than he has over an action that is deterministically inevitable; in neither case does free will enter the picture.

Immanuel Kant, print published in London, 1812. Photos.com/
Jupiterimages

Hence, if human actions are indeterministic, free will does not exist.

The German enlightenment philosopher Immanuel Kant (1724–1804), one of the earliest supporters of libertarianism, attempted to overcome the intelligibility objection, and thereby to make room for moral responsibility, by proposing a kind of dualism in human nature. In his *Critique of Practical Reason* (1788), Kant claimed that humans are free when their actions are governed by reason. Reason (what he sometimes called the "noumenal self") is in some sense independent of the rest of the agent, allowing him to choose morally. Kant's theory requires that reason be disconnected from the causal order in such a way as to be capable of choosing or acting on its own and, at the same time, that it be connected to the causal order in such a way as to be an integral determinant of human actions. The details of Kant's view have been the subject of much debate, and it remains unclear whether it is coherent.

Although libertarianism was not popular among 19th-century philosophers, it enjoyed a revival in the mid-20th century. The most influential of the new libertarian accounts were the so-called "agent-causation" theories. First proposed by the American philosopher Roderick Chisholm (1916–99) in his seminal paper "Human Freedom and the Self" (1964), these theories hold that free actions are caused by the agent himself rather than by some prior event or state of affairs. Although Chisholm's theory preserves the intuition that the ultimate origin of an action—and thus the ultimate moral responsibility for it—lies with the agent, it does not explain the details or mechanism of agent-causation. Agent-causation is a primitive, unanalyzable notion; it cannot be reduced to anything more basic. Not surprisingly, many philosophers found Chisholm's theory unsatisfactory. What is wanted, they objected, is a theory that explains what freedom is and how it is possible, not one that simply posits freedom. Agent-causation theories, they maintained, leave a blank space where an explanation ought to be.

COMPATIBILISM

Compatibilism, as the name suggests, is the view that the existence of free will and moral responsibility is compatible with the truth of determinism. In most cases compatibilists (also called "soft" determinists) attempt to achieve this reconciliation by subtly revising or weakening the commonsense notion of free will.

ANCIENT AND MEDIEVAL COMPATIBILISM

Compatibilism has an ancient history, and many philosophers have endorsed it in one form or another. In Book III of the *Nichomachean Ethics*, Aristotle (384–322 BCE) wrote that humans are responsible for the actions they freely choose to do (i.e., for their voluntary actions). While acknowledging that "our dispositions are not voluntary in the same sense that our actions are," Aristotle believed that humans have free will because they are free to choose their actions within the confines of their natures. In other words, humans are free to choose between the (limited) alternatives presented to them by their dispositions. Moreover, humans also have the special ability to mold their dispositions and to develop their moral characters. Thus, humans have freedom in two senses: they can choose between the alternatives that result from their dispositions, and they can change or develop the dispositions that present them with these alternatives. One might object that the capacity for self-examination and reflection presupposed by this kind of freedom implies the existence of something in humans that is outside the causal order. If this is so, then Aristotle's compatibilism is really a disguised form of libertarianism.

For medieval Scholastic philosophers, free will was a theological problem. If God is the prime mover—the first cause of all things and events in the universe, including human actions—and if the universe is deterministic, then it seems to follow that humans never act freely. How can humans do other than what God has caused them to do? How then can they be morally responsible for their actions? An analogous problem obtains regarding God's omniscience: if God, being omniscient, has foreknowledge of every choice that humans make, how can humans choose other than what God knows they will choose?

If there is a device in John's brain that will force him to vote for candidate B if he is inclined to vote for candidate A, but he votes for candidate B on his own, has he acted freely? Dan Kitwood/Getty Images

In late antiquity, St. Augustine (354–430) played a key role in combining Greek philosophy with Christianity, and his attempts to reconcile human freedom with Christian notions such as divine foreknowledge are still cited by theologians. According to Augustine, God—a perfect, omnipotent, and omniscient being—exists outside the realm of time. Temporal directionality does not exist for God, as it does for humans. Hence, it makes no sense to attribute foreknowledge of human choices to God.

Nearly a millennium later, St. Thomas Aquinas (c. 1224–74) grappled with the same problems. Like Augustine, he lived during a major turning point in Western intellectual history, when the relationship between philosophy and religion was being freshly examined and recast. In his *Summa theologiae* (1265/66–73), Aquinas wrote that, if humans do not have free will, all "counsels, exhortations, commands, prohibitions, rewards, and punishments would be in vain," a conclusion that is simply inconceivable. In response to the apparent conflict between freedom and God's role as the prime mover of human wills, Aquinas claimed that God is in fact the source of human freedom. This is because God moves humans "in accordance with our voluntary natures."

> *Just as by moving natural causes God does not prevent their acts being natural, so by moving voluntary causes He does not deprive their actions of being voluntary.*

Because humans are created by God, their wills are naturally in harmony with his. Thus, God's role as prime mover need not get in the way of free agency.

Modern Compatibilism

Following the rediscovery of Classical learning during the Renaissance, philosophers sympathetic to compatibilism shifted their focus from the divine back to the individual. The English philosopher Thomas Hobbes (1588–1679) argued that the only condition necessary for free will and moral responsibility is that there be a connection between one's choices and one's actions. In his *Leviathan* (1651), he asserted that free will is "the liberty of the man [to do] what he has the will, desire, or inclination to do." If a person is able to do the thing he chooses, he is free.

David Hume, another staunch compatibilist, maintained that the apparent incompatibility between determinism and free will rests on a confusion about the nature of causation. Causation is a phenomenon that humans project onto the world, he believed. To say that one thing (A) is the cause of another thing (B) is nothing more than to say that things like A have been constantly conjoined with things like B in experience, and that an observation of a thing like A inevitably brings to mind the idea or expectation of a thing like B. There is nothing in nature itself that corresponds to the "necessary connection" thought to exist between two things that are causally related. Because there is just this kind of regularity between human choices on the one hand and human actions on the other, it follows that human actions are caused by human choices, and this is all that is needed for free will. As Hume claimed in his *Enquiry Concerning Human Understanding* (1748), "By liberty we can only mean a power of acting or not acting, according to the determinations of the will."

The English philosopher John Stuart Mill (1806–73) was the major champion of compatibilism in the 19th century. He proposed that a person is free when "his habits or his temptations are not his masters, but he theirs," while an unfree person is one who obeys his desires even when he has good reason not to. Mill's position is situated at an interesting turning point in compatibilist thinking.

It echoes Kant in its reliance on reason as the vehicle of freedom, but it also anticipates contemporary compatibilism in its notion that a free person is one whose internal desires are not at odds with his reason.

In his *Ethical Studies* (1876), Mill's countryman F.H. Bradley (1846–1924) argued that neither compatibilism nor libertarianism comes close to justifying what he called the "vulgar notion" of moral responsibility. Determinism does not allow for free will because it implies that humans are never the ultimate originators of their actions. Indeterminism does no better, for it can imply only that human decisions are completely random. Yet it is intuitively obvious, according to Bradley, that humans have free will, and no philosophical argument in the world will convince anyone otherwise. He thus advocated a return to common sense. Given that the philosophical theory of determinism necessarily conflicts with people's deep-rooted moral intuitions, it is better to abandon the former rather than the latter.

Contemporary Compatibilism

Notwithstanding Bradley's argument, compatibilism remained popular among 20th-century thinkers. G.E. Moore attempted to reconcile determinism and free will through a conditional analysis of freedom. When one says that a person acted freely, according to Moore, one simply means that, if he had chosen to do otherwise, he would have done otherwise. The fact that the person may not have been in a position to choose otherwise does not undermine his free agency. But what does it mean to say that one could have done otherwise? In "Freedom and Necessity" (1946), A.J. Ayer maintained that "to say that I could have acted otherwise is to say that I should have acted otherwise if I had so chosen." The ability to do otherwise means only that, if the past had been different, one might have chosen differently. This is obviously a particularly weak notion of freedom, for it implies that a choice or action can be free even though it is completely determined by the past. It is an open question whether Ayer's account provides a satisfactory explanation of the intuitive notion of free will. Supporters maintain that this is the only type of freedom worth wanting, while detractors believe it does not come close to providing the kind of free agency that humans desire, in part because it does not imply that humans are morally responsible for their "free" actions.

Other contemporary compatibilists have attacked the hard determinist's argument at a different juncture. In an influential paper, "Alternate Possibilities and Moral Responsibility" (1969), the American philosopher Harry Frankfurt questioned whether the ability to do otherwise is truly necessary for freedom. Suppose that John is on his way to a voting booth and is undecided about whether to vote for candidate A or candidate B. Unbeknownst to him, an evil neuroscientist has implanted in John's brain a device that will, if required, fire a signal that forces John to vote for candidate B. But John decides to vote for candidate B on his own, so the device turns out to be unnecessary. The device does not fire, so John acts freely. But John could not have acted otherwise: if he had shown the slightest inclination toward candidate A, the neuroscientist's device would have made him change his mind. This "Frankfurt-style" counterexample has proved to be quite powerful in contemporary debates about free will. It demonstrates that being able to do otherwise is not necessary for free agency.

If the ability to do otherwise is not necessary, what is? Like Hobbes and Hume, Frankfurt locates freedom solely within the self. In "Freedom of the Will and the Concept of a Person" (1971), he proposed that having free will is a matter of identifying with one's desires in a certain sense. Suppose that Jack is a drug addict who wants to reform. He has a first-order desire for a certain drug, but he also has a second-order desire not to desire the drug. Although Jack does not want his first-order desire to be effective, he acts on it all the same. Because of this inner conflict, Jack is not a free agent. Now consider Jack's friend Jill, who is also a drug addict. Unlike Jack, Jill has no desire to reform. She has a first-order desire for a certain drug and a second-order desire that her first-order desire be effective. She feels no ambivalence at all about her drug addiction. Not only does she want the drug, but she also wants to want the drug. Jill identifies with her first-order desire in a way that Jack does not, and therein lies her freedom.

In "Freedom and Resentment" (1962), the English philosopher P.F. Strawson (1919–2006) introduced an influential version of compatibilism grounded in human psychology. Strawson observed that people display emotions such as resentment, anger, gratitude, and so on in response to the actions of others. He argued that holding an agent morally responsible for an action is nothing more than having such feelings, or "reactive attitudes," toward him. The question of whether the agent acts freely matters only insofar as it affects the feelings toward him that others may have. Apart from this, freedom is beside the point. Moreover, because people cannot help but feel reactive attitudes, no matter how much they may try not to, they are justified in having them, whatever the truth or falsity of determinism. (This is not to say that the specific reactive attitude a person may have on a given occasion—of blind rage as opposed to mere annoyance, for example—is always justified.)

Yet it is far from clear that people are always justified in having reactive attitudes. Pertinent information can drastically change one's feelings toward an agent. For example, a person might become less angry with a man who ran over his cat if he discovers that the man was rushing to the hospital with a desperately ill child. He may even lose his anger altogether. Given the enormous influence that everyday factual information has over what reactive attitudes people have and whether they even have them, it seems unwise to treat them as accurate barometers of moral responsibility.

CONTINUITY AND CHANGE

Although the central issues involved in the problem of moral responsibility have remained the same since ancient times, the emphasis of the debate has changed greatly. Contemporary compatibilists such as Frankfurt and Strawson tend to argue that moral responsibility has little if anything to do with determinism, because it arises from people's desires and attitudes rather than from the causal origins of their actions. Humans may not be free to as great an extent as the intuitive notion of free will suggests, but there is no other freedom to be had. Addressing the problem of moral responsibility requires establishing guidelines for holding people accountable, not lunging after some impossible notion of free will.

Contemporary libertarians such as Chisholm, however, continue to maintain that moral responsibility requires a certain kind of robust free will for which compatibilism does not allow. Their prime concern is to untangle the metaphysical issues underlying the intelligibility objection and to make room for free will in an indeterministic world.

How much of human behaviour is determined by past events, and how much does this matter—if it does matter—for free will and moral responsibility? In the end, the important question may be not whether the universe is deterministic or indeterministic but whether one is willing to accept a definition of free will that is much weaker than intuition demands.

EVOLUTIONARY ETHICS

The best known traditional form of evolutionary ethics is social Darwinism, though this view owes far more to Herbert Spencer (1820–1903) than it does to Charles Darwin (1809–82), the English naturalist who formulated the theory of evolution through natural selection. It begins with the assumption that in the natural world the struggle for existence is good, because it leads to the evolution of animals that are better adapted to their environments. From this premise it concludes that in the social world a similar struggle for existence should take place, for similar reasons. Some social Darwinists have thought that the social struggle also should be physical—taking the form of warfare, for example. More commonly, however, they assumed that the struggle should be economic, involving competition between individuals and private businesses in a legal environment of laissez faire. This was Spencer's own position.

As might be expected, not all evolutionary theorists have agreed that natural selection implies the justice of laissez-faire capitalism. Alfred Russel Wallace (1823–1913), who advocated a group-selection analysis, believed in the justice of actions that promote the welfare of the state, even at the expense of the individual, especially in cases in which the individual is already well-favoured. The Russian theorist of anarchism Peter Kropotkin (1842–1921) argued that selection proceeds through cooperation within groups ("mutual aid") rather than through struggle

Social Darwinism

Social Darwinism is the theory that persons, groups, and races are subject to the same laws of natural selection as Charles Darwin had perceived in plants and animals in nature. According to the theory, which was popular in the late 19th and early 20th centuries, the weak were diminished and their cultures delimited, while the strong grew in power and in cultural influence over the weak. Social Darwinists held that the life of humans in society is a struggle for existence ruled by "survival of the fittest," a phrase proposed by Herbert Spencer.

The social Darwinists — notably Spencer and Walter Bagehot in England and William Graham Sumner in the United States — believed that the process of natural selection acting on variations in the population would result in the survival of the best competitors and in continuing improvement in the population. Societies, like individuals, were viewed as organisms that evolve in this manner.

The theory was used to support laissez-faire capitalism and political conservatism. Class stratification was justified on the basis of "natural" inequalities among individuals, for the control of property was said to be a correlate of superior and inherent moral attributes such as industriousness, temperance, and frugality. Attempts to reform society through state intervention or other means would, therefore, interfere with natural processes. Unrestricted competition and defense of the status quo were in accord with biological selection. The poor were the "unfit" and should not be aided, whereas in the struggle for existence, wealth was a sign of success. At the societal level, social Darwinism was used as a philosophical rationalization for imperialist, colonialist, and racist policies, sustaining belief in Anglo-Saxon or "Aryan" cultural and biological superiority.

Social Darwinism declined during the 20th century as an expanded knowledge of biological, social, and cultural phenomena undermined, rather than supported, its basic tenets.

between individuals. In the 20th century, the English biologist Julian Huxley (1887–1975) — the grandson of T.H. Huxley (1825–95), who coined the term "agnosticism" — thought that the future survival of humankind, especially as the number of humans increases dramatically, would require the application of science and the undertaking of large-scale public works, such as the Tennessee Valley Authority. More recently, the biologist Edward O. Wilson has argued that, because human beings have evolved in symbiotic relationship with the rest of the living world, the supreme moral imperative is biodiversity.

From a metaethical perspective, social Darwinism was famously criticized by G.E. Moore. Invoking a line of argument first mooted by Hume, who pointed out the fallaciousness of reasoning from statements of fact to statements of moral obligation (from an "is" to an "ought"), Moore accused the social Darwinists of committing what he called the "naturalistic fallacy," the mistake of attempting to infer nonnatural properties (being morally good or right) from natural ones (the fact and processes of evolution). Evolutionary ethicists, however, were generally unmoved by this criticism, for they simply disagreed that deriving moral from nonmoral properties is always fallacious. Their confidence lay in their commitment to progress, to the belief that the products of evolution increase in moral value as the evolutionary process proceeds—from the simple to the complex, from the monad to the man, to use the traditional phrase. Another avenue of criticism of social Darwinism, therefore, was to deny that evolution is progressive in this way. T.H. Huxley pursued this line of attack, arguing that humans are imperfect in many of their biological properties and that what is morally right often contradicts humans' animal nature. In the late 20th century, the American paleontologist Stephen Jay Gould (1941–2002) made similar criticisms of attempts to derive moral precepts from the course of evolution.

The chief metaethical project in evolutionary ethics is that of understanding morality, or the moral impulse in human beings, as an evolutionary adaptation. For all the intraspecific violence that human beings commit, they are a remarkably social species, and sociality, or the capacity for cooperation, is surely adaptively valuable, even on the assumption that selection takes place solely on the level of the individual. Unlike the social insects, human beings have too variable an environment and too few offspring (requiring too much parental care) to be hard-wired for specific cooperative tasks. However, the kind of cooperative behaviour that has contributed to the survival of the species would be difficult and time-consuming to achieve through self-interested calculation by each individual. Hence, something like morality is necessary to provide a natural impulse among all individuals to cooperation and respect for the interests of others.

Although this perspective does not predict specific moral rules or values, it does suggest that some general concept of distributive justice (i.e., justice as fairness and equity) could have resulted from natural selection. This view, in fact, was endorsed by John Rawls (1921–2002). It is important to note, however, that demonstrating the evolutionary origins of any aspect of human morality does not by itself establish that the aspect is rational or correct.

An important issue in metaethics—perhaps the most important issue of all—is expressed in the question, "Why should I be moral?" What, if anything, makes it rational for an individual to behave morally (by cooperating with others) rather than purely selfishly? The present perspective suggests that moral behaviour did have an adaptive value for individuals or groups (or both) at some stages of human evolutionary history. Again, however, this fact does not imply a satisfactory answer to the moral skeptic, who claims that morality has no rational foundation

Paleontologist Stephen Jay Gould and other scientists have criticized attempts to derive moral principles from evolution. Ulf Andersen/ Getty Images

whatsoever. From the premise that morality is natural or even adaptive, it does not follow that it is rational. Nevertheless, evolutionary ethics can help to explain the persistence and near-universality of the belief that there is more to morality than mere opinion, emotion, or habit. Hume pointed out that morality would not work unless people thought of it as "real" in some sense. In the same vein, many evolutionary ethicists have argued that the belief that morality is real, though rationally unjustified, serves to make morality work. Therefore, it is adaptive. In this sense, morality may be an illusion that human beings are biologically compelled to embrace.

CHAPTER 4

APPLIED ETHICS

A pplied ethics, as the name implies, is the branch of ethics consisting of the application of normative ethical theories to practical problems. Some of the most compelling issues in contemporary applied ethics have arisen in the fields of medicine and the life sciences, where continual technological advances have created new ethical dilemmas for doctors, patients, and researchers. Another set of problems has been raised by the concern among growing numbers of people in the West about the morality of traditional ways in which humans use animals (e.g., for food, clothing, entertainment, and scientific research). The environmental movement since the 1970s, especially the emergence of global environmental issues such as ozone depletion and climate change in the late 20th century, has led to renewed speculation among philosophers about whether nonsentient living things, or the natural environment as a whole, have moral value, and if so whether inherently or by virtue of their close relation to other morally valuable things (such as future generations of humans). Finally, traditional questions regarding the morality of war and the value of peace have been especially prominent in general political discourse since the 1960s, when the morality and legality of the Vietnam War were questioned by a new generation of college students, activists, and intellectuals.

BIOETHICS

Bioethics is the branch of applied ethics that studies the philosophical, social, and legal issues arising in medicine and the life sciences. It is chiefly concerned with human life and well-being, though it sometimes also treats ethical questions relating to the nonhuman biological environment. (Such questions are studied primarily in the independent fields of environmental ethics and animal rights.)

DEFINITION AND DEVELOPMENT

The range of issues considered to fall within the purview of bioethics varies depending on how broadly the field is defined. In one common usage, bioethics is more or less equivalent to medical ethics, or biomedical ethics. The term *medical ethics* itself has been challenged, however, in light of the growing interest in issues dealing with health care professions other than medicine, in particular nursing. The professionalization of nursing and the perception of nurses as ethically accountable in their own right have led to the development of a distinct field known as nursing ethics. Accordingly, *health care ethics* has come into use as a more inclusive term. Bioethics, however, is broader than this, because some of the issues it encompasses concern not so much the practice of health care as the conduct and results of research in the life sciences, especially in areas such as cloning and gene therapy, stem cell research, xenotransplantation (animal-to-human transplantation), and human longevity.

Although bioethics—and indeed the whole field of applied ethics as currently understood—is a fairly recent phenomenon, there have been discussions of moral issues in medicine since ancient times. Examples include the corpus of the Greek physician Hippocrates (*c.* 460–*c.* 377 BCE), after whom the Hippocratic oath is named (though Hippocrates himself was not its author); the *Republic* of Plato (*c.* 428–*c.* 348 BCE), which advocates selective human breeding in anticipation of later programs of eugenics; the *Summa contra gentiles* of St. Thomas Aquinas (*c.* 1224–1274), which briefly discusses the permissibility of abortion; and the *Lectures on Ethics* of Immanuel Kant (1724-1804), which contains arguments against the sale of human body parts.

Bioethics emerged as a distinct field of study in the early 1960s. It was influenced not only by advances in the life sciences, particularly medicine, but also by the significant cultural and societal changes taking place at the time,

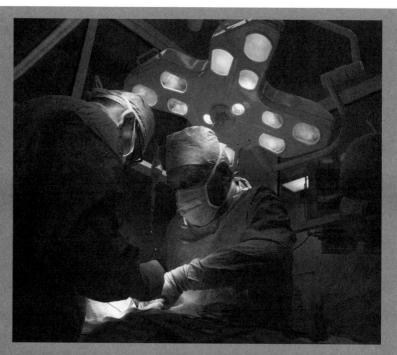

Costly and difficult procedures like organ transplantation raise the question of who should and should not receive lifesaving treatment. Christopher Furlong/Getty Images

primarily in the West. The perfection of certain lifesaving procedures and technologies, such as organ transplantation and kidney dialysis, required medical officials to make difficult decisions about which patients would receive treatment and which would be allowed to die. At the same time, the increasing importance placed on individual well-being contributed to changes in conventional attitudes toward marriage and sexuality, reproduction and child rearing, and civil rights. The ultimate result was widespread dissatisfaction with traditional medical paternalism and the gradual recognition of a patient's right to be fully informed about his condition and to retain some measure of control over what happens to his body.

ISSUES IN BIOETHICS

The issues studied in bioethics can be grouped into several categories.

THE HEALTH CARE CONTEXT

One category concerns the relationship between doctor and patient, including issues that arise from conflicts between a doctor's duty to promote the health of his patient and the patient's right to self-determination or autonomy, a right that in the medical context is usually taken to encompass a right to be fully informed about one's condition and a right to be consulted about the course of one's treatment. Is a doctor obliged to tell a patient that he is terminally ill if there is good reason to believe that doing so would hasten the patient's death? If a patient with a life-threatening illness refuses treatment, should his wishes be respected? Should patients always be permitted to refuse the use of extraordinary life-support measures? These questions become more complicated when the patient is incapable of making rational decisions in his own interest,

as in the case of infants and children, patients suffering
from disabling psychiatric disorders such as schizophrenia
or degenerative brain diseases such as Alzheimer disease,
and patients who are in a vegetative state.

TRADITIONAL PHILOSOPHICAL QUESTIONS

Another category of issues concerns a host of philosophical questions about the definition and significance of life
and death, the nature of personhood and identity, and the
extent of human freedom and individual responsibility. At
what point should a fatally injured or terminally ill patient
be considered dead? When his vital functions (e.g., heart-
beat and breathing) have ceased? When the brain stem has
ceased to function? Should the presence of deep coma be
sufficient to establish death? These and similar questions
were given new urgency in the 1960s, when the increased
demand for human organs and tissues for use in transplant
operations forced medical ethicists to establish guidelines
for determining when it is permissible to remove organs
from a potential donor.

At about the same time, the development of safer
techniques of surgical abortion and the growing accept-
ability of abortion as a method of birth control prompted
increasing debate about the moral status of the human
fetus. In philosophical discussion, this debate was framed
in terms of the notion of a "person," understood as any
being whose interests are deserving of special moral concern. The central issue was whether—and, if so, at what
stage—the fetus is a person in the moral sense. In slightly
different terms, the issue was whether the class of persons
is coextensive with the class of human beings—whether
all and only human beings are persons, or whether instead
there can be human beings who are not persons or persons
who are not human beings (the latter category, according to some, includes some of the higher animals and

hypothetical creatures such as intelligent Martians). These questions were raised anew in later decades in response to the development of drugs, such as RU-486 (mifepristone), that induce abortion up to several weeks after conception and to the use of stem cells taken from human embryos in research on the treatment of conditions such as parkinsonism (Parkinson disease) and injuries of the central nervous system.

A closely related set of issues concerns the nature of personal identity. Recent advances in techniques of cloning, which enabled the successful cloning of animals such as sheep and rabbits, have renewed discussion of the traditional philosophical question of what, if anything, makes a particular human being the unique person he is. Is a person just the sum of the information encoded in his genes? If so, is the patient who has undergone gene therapy a different person from the one he was before (i.e., has he become someone else)? If a human being were to be cloned, in what sense would he be a copy of his "parent"? Would he and his parent be the same person? If multiple human beings were cloned from the same parent, would they and their parent all be the same person?

The attempt to understand personal identity in terms of genetic information also raised anew the philosophical problems of free will and determinism. To what extent, if any, is human personality or character genetically rather than environmentally determined? Are there genetic bases for certain types of behaviour, as there seem to be for certain types of diseases (e.g., Tay-Sachs disease)? If so, what kinds of behaviour are so influenced, and to what extent are they also influenced by environmental factors? If behaviour is at least partly genetically determined, should individuals always be held fully responsible for what they do?

Finally, the possibility of developing technologies that would extend the human life span far beyond its current natural length, if not indefinitely, has led to speculation about the value of life, the significance of death, and the desirability of immortality. Is life intrinsically valuable? In cases in which one is not suffering physically or emotionally, is it always better to be alive than dead? If so, is it rational to desire immortality? What would be the significance of death in a world in which dying was not biologically inevitable?

SOCIAL AND LEGAL ISSUES

Many of these philosophical questions, however they are answered, have significant social and legal dimensions. For example, advances in medical technology have the potential to create disproportionate disadvantages for some social groups, either by being applied in ways that harm members of the groups directly or by encouraging the adoption of social policies that discriminate unfairly against them. Accordingly, questions of discrimination in bioethics have arisen in a number of areas. In one such area, reproductive medicine, recently developed techniques have enabled parents to choose the sex of their child. Should this new power be considered liberating or oppressive? Would it be viewed positively if the vast majority of the parents who use it choose to have a boy rather than a girl? Similar concerns have been raised about the increasing use of abortion as a method of birth control in overpopulated countries such as India and China, where there is considerable social and legal pressure to limit family size and where male children are valued more highly than female children.

In the field of genetics, the use of relatively simple tests for determining a patient's susceptibility to certain genetically transmitted diseases has led to concerns in the United States and other countries that the results of such tests, if not properly safeguarded, could be used in unfair ways by health-insurance companies, employers, and government agencies. In addition, the advent of so-called "genetic counseling"—in which prospective parents receive advice about the chances that their offspring will inherit a certain genetic disease or disorder—has allowed couples to make more informed decisions about reproduction but also has contributed, in the view of some bioethicists, to a social atmosphere considerably less tolerant of disability than it ought to be. The same criticism has been leveled against the practice of diagnosing, and in some cases treating, congenital defects in unborn children.

Research on the genetic bases of behaviour, though still in its infancy, is controversial, and it has even been criticized as scientifically invalid. Whatever its scientific merits, however, it has the potential, according to some bioethicists, to encourage the adoption of crude models of genetic determinism in the development of social policies, especially in the areas of education and crime prevention. Such policies, it is claimed, could result in unfair discrimination against large numbers of people judged to be genetically disposed to "undesirable" forms of behaviour, such as aggression or violence.

This last point suggests a related set of issues concerning the moral status of scientific inquiry itself. The notion that there is a clear line between, on the one hand, the discovery and presentation of scientific facts and, on the other, the discussion of moral issues—the idea that moral issues arise only after scientific research is concluded—is now widely regarded as mistaken. Science is not value-neutral. Indeed, there have been ethical debates about whether certain kinds of research should be undertaken at all, irrespective of their possible applications. It has been argued, for example, that research on the possible genetic basis of homosexuality is immoral, because even the assumption that such a basis exists implicitly characterizes homosexuality as a kind of genetic abnormality. In any case, it is plausible to suggest that scientific research should always be informed by philosophy—in particular by ethics but also, arguably, by the philosophy of mind. Consideration of the moral issues related to one particular branch of medicine, namely psychiatry, makes it clear that such issues arise not only in areas of treatment but also in matters of diagnosis and classification, where the application of labels indicating illness or abnormality may create serious disadvantages for the individuals so designated.

Many of the moral issues that have arisen in the health care context and in the wake of advances in medical technology have been addressed, in whole or in part, in legislation. It is important to realize, however, that the content of such legislation is seldom, if ever, dictated by the positions one takes on particular moral issues. For example, the view that voluntary euthanasia is morally permissible in certain circumstances does not by itself settle the question of whether euthanasia should be legalized. The possibility of legalization carries with it another set of issues, such as the potential for abuse. Some bioethicists have expressed the concern that the legalization of euthanasia would create a perception among some elderly patients that society expects them to request euthanasia, even if they do not desire it, in order not to be a burden to others. Similarly, even those who believe that abortion is morally permissible in certain circumstances may consistently object to proposals to relax or eliminate laws against it.

A final class of social and legal questions concerns the allocation of health care resources. The issue of whether health care should be primarily an individual or a public responsibility remains deeply controversial. Although systems of health care allocation differ widely, they all face the problem that resources are scarce and consequently expensive. Debate has focused not only on the relative cost-effectiveness of different systems but also on the different conceptions of justice that underlie them. The global allocation of health care resources, including generic forms of drugs for life-threatening illnesses such as HIV/AIDS, is an important topic in the field of developing world bioethics.

APPROACHES

Bioethics is a branch of applied ethics. To say that it is "applied," however, does not imply that it presupposes any particular ethical theory. Contemporary bioethicists make use of a variety of different views, including primarily utilitarianism and Kantianism but also more recently developed perspectives such as virtue theory and perspectives drawn from philosophical feminism, particularly the school of thought known as the ethics of care.

TRADITIONAL AND CONTEMPORARY ETHICAL THEORIES

Utilitarianism is a normative-ethical theory that holds that the moral rightness or wrongness of an action should be ascertained in terms of the action's consequences. According to one common formulation, an action is right if it would promote a greater amount of happiness for a greater number of people than would any other action performable in the same circumstances. The Kantian tradition, in contrast, eschews the notion of consequences and urges instead that an action is right only if it is universalizable (i.e., only if the moral rule it embodies could become a universal law applicable to all moral agents). The Kantian approach emphasizes respect for the individual, autonomy, dignity, and human rights.

Unlike these traditional approaches, both virtue ethics and the ethics of care focus on dimensions of moral theorizing other than determining the rightness or wrongness of particular actions. Virtue ethics is concerned with the nature of moral character and with the traits, capacities, or dispositions that moral agents ought to cultivate in themselves and others. Thus, the virtue ethicist may consider what character traits, such as compassion and courage, are desirable in a doctor, nurse, or biomedical researcher and how they would (or should) be manifested in various settings. The basic aim of the ethics of care is to replace—or at least augment—the supposedly "masculine" moral values of rationality, abstraction, impartiality, and independence with ostensibly more "feminine" values, such as emotion (particularly compassion and benevolence), particularity, partiality, and interdependence. From this perspective, reflection on abortion would begin not with abstract principles such as the right to autonomy or the right to life but with considerations of the needs of women who face the choice of whether to have an abortion and the particular ways in which their decisions may affect their lives and the lives of their families. This approach also would address social and legal aspects of the abortion debate, such as the fact that, though abortion affects the lives of women much more directly than it does the lives of men, women as a group are significantly underrepresented in the institutions that create abortion-related laws and regulations.

THE FOUR-PRINCIPLES APPROACH

Whereas some approaches in bioethics proceed by applying principles derived from independent ethical theories to individual cases (a "top-down" approach), others proceed by examining individual cases to elucidate the principles that seem to guide most people's thinking about bioethical issues in actual practice (a "bottom-up" approach).

One influential approach along these lines, known as the "four principles" of bioethics, attempts to describe a set of minimum moral conditions on the behaviour of health care professionals. The first principle, autonomy, entails that health care professionals should respect the autonomous decisions of competent adults. The second principle, beneficence, holds that they should aim to do good (i.e., to promote the interests of their patients). The third principle, nonmaleficence, requires that they should do no harm. Finally, the fourth principle, justice, holds that they should act fairly when the interests of different individuals or groups are in competition (e.g., by promoting the fair allocation of health care resources).

According to proponents of the four-principles approach, one of its advantages is that, because the principles are independent of any particular ethical theory, they can be used by theorists working in a variety of different traditions. Both the utilitarian and the Kantian, it is argued, can support the principle of autonomy, though they would do so for different reasons. Nevertheless, this adaptability may also be construed as a disadvantage. Critics have contended that the principles are so general that whatever agreement on them there may be is unlikely to be very meaningful. Thus, although the utilitarian and the Kantian may both accept the principle of autonomy, the principle as it is formulated allows them to understand the notion of autonomy in very different ways. Another criticism of the approach is that it does not offer any clear way of prioritizing between the principles in cases where they conflict—as they are often liable to do. The principle of autonomy, for example, might conflict with the principle of beneficence in cases where a competent adult patient refuses to accept life-saving treatment.

Despite these problems, the principles remain useful as a framework in which to think about moral issues in medicine and the life sciences. This is not an inconsiderable contribution, for, on at least one conception of the field, the main task of bioethics is not so much to provide answers to moral problems as to identify where the problems lie.

THE SIGNIFICANCE OF PUBLIC ATTITUDES

Since its inception the field of bioethics has been populated by specialists from a number of different disciplines, including primarily philosophers, lawyers, and theologians. In the last decade of the 20th century, however, the contributions of social scientists to bioethical research became particularly important. Work of this type involved surveys of public attitudes to advances in the life sciences, including xenotransplantation and genetic modification. Programs for facilitating public understanding of these advances were developed, leading to the establishment of "public understanding" and later "public engagement," or "participation," as distinct topics of study in bioethics and the social sciences.

These topics have been important from both a practical and a theoretical point of view. In order to formulate sound public policies on issues such as human cloning, for example, it is important to be able to predict how such technology, were it to become widely available, would affect the public's decision making about reproduction. At the same time, research on public attitudes may reveal that some bioethical principles, such as the principle of autonomy, may not be suitable for some societies, particularly those with cultures that are not particularly individualistic. For these societies, something like a "principle of solidarity" may have greater relevance. Nevertheless, it would be a mistake to assume that one of these principles must apply to the exclusion of the other—it is possible for a society to value both autonomy and solidarity.

Policy Making

The importance of the social and legal issues addressed in bioethics is reflected in the large number of national and international bodies established to advise governments on appropriate public policy. At the national level, several countries have set up bioethics councils or commissions. Elsewhere, as in the United Kingdom, there are a variety of different bodies that consider bioethical issues as well as national bodies that deal with specific fields.

Several international organizations also are involved in policy making on bioethical issues. The United Nations Educational, Scientific and Cultural Organization (UNESCO), for example, has an International Bioethics Committee; the Human Genome Organisation has an Ethics Committee; and the Council of Europe has issued the Convention on Human Rights and Biomedicine. The proliferation of such committees is evidence of the increasing political influence of the work performed by bioethicists. Indeed, acquaintance with developments in bioethics arguably is becoming an important aspect of national and global citizenship. At the same time, however, the role of bioethical experts on advisory or decision-making bodies has itself become a topic of study in bioethics.

Global Bioethics

The field of bioethics has grown most rapidly in North America, Australia and New Zealand, and Europe. Cross-cultural discussion also has expanded and in 1992 led to the establishment of the International Association of Bioethics. A significant discussion under way since the start of the 21st century has concerned the possibility of a "global" bioethics that would be capable of encompassing the values and cultural traditions of non-Western societies. Some bioethicists maintain that a global bioethics could be founded on the four-principles approach, in view of its apparent compatibility with widely differing ethical theories and worldviews. Others argue to the contrary that the four principles are not an appropriate basis for a global bioethics because at least some of them—in particular the principle of autonomy—reflect peculiarly Western values. Although the issue remains unresolved, the field as a whole continues to grow in sophistication. At the same time, the increasing pace of technological advances in medicine and the life sciences demands that bioethicists continually rethink the basic assumptions of their field and reflect carefully on their own methodologies.

ANIMAL RIGHTS

Animal rights are moral or legal entitlements that are attributed to some nonhuman animals, usually because of the complexity of their cognitive, emotional, and social lives or their capacity to experience physical or emotional pain and pleasure. Historically, different views of the scope of animal rights have reflected philosophical and legal developments, scientific conceptions of animal and human nature, and religious and ethical conceptions of the proper relationship between animals and human beings.

HISTORICAL BACKGROUND: VEGETARIANISM FROM ANTIQUITY TO THE PRESENT

Philosophical and religious speculation about the moral status of nonhuman animals is certainly not unique to the present day. In many cultures and in many eras since ancient times, doctrines about the divine creation of animal and human life, the nature of the human soul, the moral value of pleasure and pain, and the obligations of sympathy and benevolence toward other beings have motivated people to advocate more humane ways of treating animals. The practical consequences of these doctrines are no better illustrated than in the ancient and widespread practice of vegetarianism.

Vegetarianism is the theory or practice of living solely upon vegetables, fruits, grains, and nuts—with or without the addition of milk products and eggs—generally for ethical, ascetic, environmental, or nutritional reasons. All forms of flesh (meat, fowl, and seafood) are excluded from all vegetarian diets, but many vegetarians use milk and milk products. Westerner vegetarians usually eat eggs also, but most vegetarians in India exclude them, as did those in the Mediterranean lands in Classical times. Vegetarians who exclude animal products altogether (and likewise avoid animal-derived products such as leather, silk, and wool) are known as vegans. Those who use milk products are sometimes called lacto-vegetarians, and those who use eggs as well are called lacto-ovo vegetarians. Among some agricultural peoples, flesh eating has been infrequent except among the privileged classes. Such people have rather misleadingly been called vegetarians.

ANCIENT ORIGINS

Deliberate avoidance of flesh eating probably first appeared sporadically in ritual connections, either as a temporary purification or as qualification for a priestly function. Advocacy of a regular fleshless diet began about the middle of the 1st millennium BCE in India and the eastern Mediterranean as part of the philosophical awakening of the time. In the Mediterranean, avoidance of flesh eating is first recorded as a teaching of the philosopher Pythagoras of Samos (c. 580–c. 500 BCE), who alleged the kinship of all animals as one basis for human benevolence toward other creatures. From Plato onward many pagan philosophers, especially the Neoplatonists, recommended a fleshless diet; the idea carried with it condemnation of bloody sacrifices in worship and was often associated with belief in the reincarnation of souls and, more generally, with a search for principles of cosmic harmony in accord with which human beings could live. In India, followers of Buddhism and Jainism refused on ethical and ascetic grounds to kill animals for food. Human beings, they believed, should not inflict harm on any sentient creature. This principle was soon taken up in Brahmanism and, later, Hinduism and was applied especially to the cow. As in Mediterranean thought, the idea carried with it condemnation of bloody sacrifices and was often associated with principles of cosmic harmony.

In later centuries the history of vegetarianism in the Indic and Mediterranean regions diverged significantly. In India itself, though Buddhism gradually declined, the ideal of harmlessness (ahimsa), with its corollary of a fleshless diet, spread steadily in the 1st millennium CE until many of the upper castes, and even some of the lower, had adopted it. Beyond India it was carried, with Buddhism, northward and eastward as far as China and Japan. In some countries, fish were included in an otherwise fleshless diet.

West of the Indus the great monotheistic traditions were less favourable to vegetarianism. The Hebrew Bible, however, records the belief that in paradise the earliest human beings had not eaten flesh. Ascetic Jewish groups and some early Christian leaders disapproved of flesh eating as gluttonous, cruel, and expensive. Some Christian monastic orders ruled out flesh eating, and its avoidance has been a penance and a spiritual exercise even for laypersons. Many Muslims have been hostile to vegetarianism, yet some Muslim Sufi mystics recommended a meatless diet for spiritual seekers.

THE 17TH THROUGH 19TH CENTURIES

The 17th and 18th centuries in Europe were characterized by a greater interest in humanitarianism and the idea of moral progress, and sensitivity to animal suffering was accordingly revived. Certain Protestant groups came to adopt a fleshless diet as part of the goal of leading a perfectly sinless life. Persons of diverse philosophical views advocated vegetarianism. For example, Voltaire (1694–1778) praised it, and Percy Bysshe Shelley (1792–1822) and Henry David Thoreau (1817–62) practiced the diet. In the late 18th century Jeremy Bentham (1748–1832) asserted that the suffering of animals, like the suffering of humans, was worthy of moral consideration, and he regarded cruelty to animals as analogous to racism.

Vegetarians of the early 19th century usually condemned the use of alcohol as well as flesh and appealed as much to nutritional advantages as to ethical sensibilities. As before, vegetarianism tended to be combined with other efforts toward a humane and cosmically harmonious way of life. Although the vegetarian movement as a whole was always carried forward by ethically inclined individuals, special institutions grew up to express vegetarian concerns as such. The first vegetarian society was formed in England in 1847 by the Bible Christian sect, and the International Vegetarian Union was founded tentatively in 1889 and more enduringly in 1908.

MODERN DEVELOPMENTS

By the early 20th century vegetarianism in the West was contributing substantially to the drive to vary and lighten the nonvegetarian diet. In some places a fleshless diet was regarded as a regimen for specific disorders. Elsewhere, notably in Germany, it was considered as one element in a wider conception of vegetarianism, which involved a comprehensive reform of life habits in the direction of simplicity and healthfulness.

In the second half of the 20th century, the work of the Australian ethical philosopher Peter Singer inspired a revival of philosophical interest in the practice of vegetarianism and the larger topic of animal rights. Singer offered utilitarian arguments to support his contention that modern methods of raising and slaughtering animals for human food ("factory farming") are morally unjustified. His arguments also applied to other traditional ways in which humans use animals, including as experimental subjects in medical research and as sources of entertainment. Singer's work provoked much vexed discussion of the question of whether the traditional treatment of animals is justified by any "morally relevant" differences between animals and humans.

Meanwhile, other debates centred on the question of whether a fleshless diet, and specifically a vegan one, provides all the nutrients necessary for human health. In the West, for example, it was long a common belief that humans cannot obtain enough protein from a diet based solely on plant foods. However, nutritional studies conducted in the 1970s cast doubt on this claim, and it is seldom advanced today. A more recent issue is whether a vegan diet can provide enough vitamin B_{12}, which humans need in tiny amounts (1 to 3 micrograms per day) to produce red blood cells and to maintain proper nerve functioning. Popular vegan sources of B_{12} include nutritional yeast, certain fortified foods made without animal products (such as cereals and soy milk), and vitamin supplements.

By the early 21st century vegetarian restaurants were commonplace in many Western countries, and large industries were devoted to producing special vegetarian and vegan foods (some of which were designed to simulate various kinds of flesh and dairy products in form and flavour).

Today many vegetarian societies and animal rights groups publish vegetarian recipes and other information on what they consider to be the health and environmental benefits, as well as the moral virtues, of a fleshless diet.

PHILOSOPHICAL BACKGROUND

The proper treatment of animals is a very old question in the West. Ancient Greek and Roman philosophers debated the place of animals in human morality. As noted earlier, the Pythagoreans and the Neoplatonists urged respect for animals' interests, primarily because they believed in the transmigration of souls between human and animal bodies. In his biological writings, Aristotle (384–322 BCE) repeatedly suggested that animals lived for their own sake, but his claim in the *Politics* that nature made all animals for the sake of humans was unfortunately destined to become his most influential statement on the subject.

Aristotle, and later the Stoics, believed the world was populated by an infinity of beings arranged hierarchically according to their complexity and perfection, from the barely living to the merely sentient, the rational, and the wholly spiritual. In this Great Chain of Being, as it came to be known, all forms of life were represented as existing for the sake of those forms higher in the chain. Among corporeal beings, humans, by dint of their rationality, occupied the highest position. The Great Chain of Being became one of the most persistent and powerful, if utterly erroneous, ways of conceiving the universe, dominating scientific, philosophical, and religious thinking until the middle of the 19th century.

The Stoics, insisting on the irrationality of all non-human animals, regarded them as slaves and accordingly treated them as contemptible and beneath notice. Aggressively advocated by St. Augustine (354–430), these

Stoic ideas became embedded in Christian theology. They were absorbed wholesale into Roman law—as reflected in the treatises and codifications of Gaius (fl. 130–180) and Justinian (483–565)—taken up by the legal glossators of Europe in the 11th century, and eventually pressed into English (and, much later, American) common law. Meanwhile, arguments that urged respect for the interests of animals nearly disappeared, and animal welfare remained a relative backwater of philosophical inquiry and legal regulation until the final decades of the 20th century.

ANIMALS AND THE LAW

In the 3rd or 4th century CE, the Roman jurist Hermogenianus wrote, "Hominum causa omne jus constitum" ("All law was established for men's sake"). Repeating the phrase, P.A. Fitzgerald's 1966 treatise *Salmond on Jurisprudence* declared, "The law is made for men and allows no fellowship or bonds of obligation between them and the lower animals." The most important consequence of this view is that animals have long been categorized as "legal things," not as "legal persons." Whereas legal persons have rights of their own, legal things do not. They exist in the law solely as the objects of the rights of legal persons (e.g., as things over which legal persons may exercise property rights). This status, however, often affords animals the indirect protection of laws intended to preserve social morality or the rights of animal owners, such as criminal anticruelty statutes or civil statutes that permit owners to obtain compensation for damages inflicted on their animals. Indeed, this sort of law presently defines the field of "animal law," which is much broader than animal rights because it encompasses all law that addresses the interests of nonhuman animals—or, more commonly, the interests of the people who own them.

A legal thing can become a legal person; this happened whenever human slaves were freed. The former legal thing then possesses his own legal rights and remedies. Parallels have frequently been drawn between the legal status of animals and that of human slaves. "The truly striking fact about slavery," the American historian David Brion Davis has written, is the

> *antiquity and almost universal acceptance of the concept of the slave as a human being who is legally owned, used, sold, or otherwise disposed of as if he or she were a domestic animal. This parallel persisted in the similarity of naming slaves, branding them, and even pricing them according to their equivalent in cows, camels, pigs, and chickens.*

The American jurist Roscoe Pound (1870–1964) wrote that in ancient Rome a slave "was a thing, and as such, like animals could be the object of rights of property." In the late 18th and early 19th centuries, humanitarian reformers in Britain and the United States campaigned on behalf of the weak and defenseless, protesting against child labour, debtor's prisons, abusive punishment in public schools, and, inevitably, the cruel treatment of animals. In 1800 the most renowned abolitionist of the period, William Wilberforce (1759–1833), supported a bill to abolish bull- and bearbaiting, which was defeated in the House of Commons. In 1809 Baron Erskine (1750–1823), former lord chancellor of England, who had long been troubled by cruelty to animals, introduced a bill to prohibit cruelty to all domestic animals. Erskine declared that the bill was intended to "consecrate, perhaps, in all nations, and in all ages, that just and eternal principle which binds the whole living world in one harmonious chain, under the dominion of enlightened man, the lord and governor of all." Although the bill passed the House of Lords, it failed in the House of Commons. Then, in 1821, a bill "to prevent cruel and improper treatment of Cattle" was introduced in the House of Commons, sponsored by Wilberforce and Thomas Fowell Buxton (1786–1845) and championed by Irish member of Parliament Richard Martin. The version enacted in 1822, known as Martin's Act, made it a crime to treat a handful of domesticated animals—cattle, oxen, horses, and sheep—cruelly or to inflict unnecessary suffering upon them. However, it did not protect the general welfare of even these animals, much less give them legal rights, and the worst punishment available for any breach was a modest fine. Similar statutes were enacted in all the states of the United States, where there now exists a patchwork of anticruelty and animal-welfare laws. Most states today make at least some abuses of animals a felony. Laws such as the federal Animal Welfare Act (1966), for example, regulate what humans may do to animals in agriculture, biomedical research, entertainment, and other areas. But neither Martin's Act nor many subsequent animal-protection statutes altered the traditional legal status of animals as legal things.

This situation changed in 2008, when the Spanish national parliament adopted resolutions urging the government to grant orangutans, chimpanzees, and gorillas some statutory rights previously afforded only to humans. The resolutions also called for banning the use of apes in performances, harmful research, and trading as well as in other practices that involve profiting from the animals. Although zoos would still be allowed to hold apes, they would be required to provide them with "optimal" living conditions.

THE MODERN ANIMAL RIGHTS MOVEMENT

The fundamental principle of the modern animal rights movement is that many nonhuman animals have basic interests that deserve recognition, consideration, and protection. In the view of animal rights advocates, these basic interests give the animals that have them both moral and legal rights.

It has been said that the modern animal rights movement is the first social reform movement initiated by philosophers. Peter Singer and the American philosopher Tom Regan deserve special mention, not just because their work has been influential but because they represent two major currents of philosophical thought regarding the moral rights of animals. Singer, whose book *Animal Liberation* (1972) is considered one of the movement's foundational documents, argues that the interests of humans and the interests of animals should be given equal consideration. A utilitarian, Singer holds that actions are morally right to the extent that they maximize pleasure or minimize pain. The key consideration is whether an animal is sentient and can therefore suffer pain or experience pleasure. This point was emphasized by Bentham, who wrote of animals, "The question is not, Can they *reason?*, nor, Can they *talk?* but, Can they *suffer?*" Given that animals can suffer, Singer argues, humans have a moral obligation to minimize or avoid causing such suffering, just as they have an obligation to minimize or avoid causing the suffering of other humans. Regan, who is not a utilitarian, argues that at least some animals have basic moral rights because they possess the same advanced cognitive abilities that justify the attribution of basic moral rights to humans. By virtue of these abilities, these animals have not just instrumental but inherent value. In Regan's words, they are "the subject of a life."

Regan, Singer, and other philosophical proponents of animal rights have encountered resistance. Some religious authors argue that animals are not as deserving of moral consideration as humans are because only humans possess an immortal soul. Others claim, as did the Stoics, that because animals are irrational, humans have no duties toward them. Still others locate the morally relevant difference between humans and animals in the ability to talk, the possession of free will, or membership in a moral community (a community whose members are capable of acting morally or immorally). The problem with these counterarguments is that, with the exception of the theological argument—which cannot be demonstrated—none differentiates all humans from all animals.

While philosophers catalyzed the modern animal rights movement, they were soon joined by physicians, writers, scientists, academics, lawyers, theologians, psychologists, nurses, veterinarians, and other professionals, who worked within their own fields to promote animal rights. Many professional organizations were established to educate colleagues and the general public regarding the exploitation of animals.

At the beginning of the 21st century, lawsuits in the interests of nonhuman animals, sometimes with nonhuman animals named as plaintiffs, became common. Given the key positions that lawyers hold in the creation of public policy and the protection of rights, their increasing interest in animal rights and animal-protection issues was significant. Dozens of law schools in Europe, the United States, and elsewhere offered courses in animal law and animal rights; the Animal Legal Defense Fund had created an even greater number of law-student chapters in the United States; and at least three legal journals—*Animal Law*, *Journal of Animal Law*, and *Journal of Animal Law and Ethics*—had been established. Legal scholars were devising and evaluating theories by which nonhuman animals would possess basic legal rights, often for the same reasons as humans do and on the basis of the same legal principles and values. These arguments were powerfully assisted by increasingly sophisticated scientific investigations into the cognitive, emotional, and social capacities of animals and by advances in genetics, neuroscience, physiology, linguistics, psychology, evolution, and ethology, many of which have demonstrated that humans and animals share a broad range of behaviours, capacities, and genetic material.

Meanwhile, the increasingly systemic and brutal abuses of animals in modern society—by the billions on factory farms and by the tens of millions in biomedical-research laboratories—spawned thousands of animal rights groups. Some consisted of a mere handful of people interested in local, and more traditional, animal-protection issues, such as animal shelters that care for stray dogs and cats. Others became large national and international organizations, such as PETA (People for the

Individuals as well as larger organizations such as the Humane Society of the United States, are demanding that government do more to protect animals. Kris Connor/Getty Images

Ethical Treatment of Animals) and the Humane Society of the United States, which in the early 21st century had millions of members and a multimillion-dollar annual budget. In all their manifestations, animal rights groups began to inundate legislatures with demands for regulation and reform.

Slaves, human and nonhuman, may be indirectly protected through laws intended to protect others. But they remain invisible to civil law, for they have no rights to protect directly until their legal personhood is recognized. This recognition can occur in a variety of ways. British slavery was abolished by judicial decision in the 18th century, and slavery in the British colonies was ended by statute early in the 19th century. By constitutional amendment, the United States ended slavery three decades later. Legal personhood for some animals may be obtained through any of these routes. The first serious direct judicial challenges to the legal thinghood of nonhuman animals may be just a few years away.

Speciesism

"Speciesism" is a term that some advocates of animal rights have applied to the practice of favouring the interests of humans over the similar interests of other species. It is also used to refer to the belief that this practice is justified. The inventor of the notion, the English philosopher Richard Ryder, and others, notably Peter Singer, have claimed that speciesism is exactly analogous to racism, sexism, and all other forms of discrimination and prejudice.

An influential argument against the legitimacy of speciesism, due to Singer, rests on the principle of equal consideration of interests (PEC). This is the claim that one should give equal weight in one's moral decision making to the similar interests of all those affected by one's actions. According to Singer, the PEC expresses what most people since the 20th century would understand (upon reflection) by the idea of human equality. The PEC implies, among other things, that one should not give greater weight to the interests of whites or males than one does to the similar interests of blacks or females. Race and sex, in other words, are morally irrelevant characteristics when it comes to evaluating the similar interests of different persons.

According to Singer, anyone who accepts the PEC must agree that a broader version of the principle applies to animals as well as to humans. If the PEC were restricted to humans, species would count as a morally relevant characteristic on the basis of which one could treat the interests of one kind of being as more important than the similar interests of another. But it is unclear why species should have this special status. There is no good reason to suppose that it is any more relevant than race or sex. If this is correct, speciesism is just as immoral as racism and sexism, and for the same reasons.

Most philosophers who reject this line of thinking have tried to show that species is a morally relevant characteristic because it is uniquely associated with one or more capabilities (e.g., rationality) that are themselves morally relevant. Because, according to speciesists, all humans and no animals have these capabilities, the PEC applies only to humans, and speciesism is not equivalent to racism and sexism.

One difficulty with this response is that it is not obvious why rationality or any other proposed capability should be considered morally relevant (i.e., why it should count as a reason for favouring the interests of any being). The main objection, however, is that for each of the proposed capabilities there are counterexamples based on so-called "marginal cases." It is clear, for example, that some humans—including infants and the profoundly mentally retarded—are not rational. It is also clear that some animals are rational, if by rationality one understands the ability to adapt means to ends in novel ways. The defender of speciesism thus faces a dilemma: either the interests of humans are no more important than the similar interests of animals, or the interests of some animals are just as important as the similar interests of humans.

Speciesists have replied to marginal-case objections in various ways, none of which has won general acceptance.

ENVIRONMENTAL ETHICS

Environmental ethics is the field of applied ethics that considers questions concerning human moral obligations to the natural environment. Two schools of thought, corresponding to two broad intellectual camps within the environmental movement, emerged in the second half of the 20th century: "anthropocentric," or "human-centred," ethics and "biocentric," or "life-centred," ethics. This division has been described in other terminology as "shallow" ecology versus "deep" ecology and as "technocentrism" versus "ecocentrism." Anthropocentric approaches focus mainly on the negative effects that environmental degradation has on human beings and their interests, including their interests in health, recreation, and quality of life. It is often characterized by a mechanistic approach to nonhuman nature in which individual creatures and species have only an instrumental value for humans. The defining feature of anthropocentrism is that it considers the moral obligations humans have to the environment to derive from obligations that humans have to each other—and, less crucially, to future generations of humans—rather than from any obligation to other living things or to the environment as a whole. Human obligations to the environment are thus indirect.

Critics of anthropocentrism have charged that it amounts to a form of human "chauvinism." They argue that anthropocentric approaches presuppose the historically Western view of nature as merely a resource to be managed or exploited for human purposes—a view that they claim is responsible for centuries of environmental destruction. In contrast to anthropocentrism, biocentrism claims that nature has an intrinsic moral worth that does not depend on its usefulness to human beings, and it is this intrinsic worth that gives rise directly to obligations to the environment. Humans are therefore morally bound to protect the environment, as well as individual creatures and species, for their own sake. In this sense, biocentrics view human beings and other elements of the natural environment, both living and often nonliving, as members of a single moral and ecological community.

By the 1960s and '70s, as scientific knowledge of the causes and consequences of environmental degradation was becoming more extensive and sophisticated, there was increasing concern among some scientists, intellectuals, and activists about the Earth's ability to absorb the detritus of human economic activity and, indeed, to sustain human life. This concern contributed to the growth of grassroots environmental activism in a number of countries, the establishment of new environmental nongovernmental organizations, and the formation of environmental ("green") political parties in a number of Western democracies. As political leaders gradually came to appreciate the seriousness of environmental problems, governments entered into negotiations in the early 1970s that led to the adoption of a growing number of international environmental agreements.

The division between anthropocentric and biocentric approaches played a central role in the development of environmental thought in the late 20th century. Whereas some earlier schools, such as apocalyptic (survivalist) environmentalism and emancipatory environmentalism—as well as its offshoot, human-welfare ecology—were animated primarily by a concern for human well-being, later movements, including social ecology, deep ecology, the animal-rights and animal-liberation movements, and ecofeminism, were centrally concerned with the moral worth of nonhuman nature.

Anthropocentric Schools of Thought

The vision of the environmental movement of the 1960s and early '70s was generally pessimistic, reflecting a pervasive sense of "civilization malaise" and a conviction that the Earth's long-term prospects were bleak. Works such as Rachel Carson's *Silent Spring* (1962), Garrett Hardin's "The Tragedy of the Commons" (1968), Paul Ehrlich's *The Population Bomb* (1968), Donella H. Meadows's *The Limits to Growth* (1972), and Edward Goldsmith's *Blueprint for Survival* (1972) suggested that the planetary ecosystem was reaching the limits of what it could sustain. This so-called apocalyptic, or survivalist, literature encouraged reluctant calls from some environmentalists for increasing the powers of centralized governments over human activities deemed environmentally harmful, a viewpoint expressed most vividly in Robert Heilbroner's *An Inquiry into the Human Prospect* (1974), which argued that human survival ultimately required the sacrifice of human freedom. Counterarguments, such as those presented in Julian Simon and Herman Kahn's *The Resourceful Earth* (1984), emphasized humanity's ability to find or to invent substitutes for resources that were scarce and in danger of being exhausted.

Beginning in the 1970s, many environmentalists attempted to develop strategies for limiting environmental degradation through recycling, the use of alternative-energy technologies, the decentralization and democratization of economic and social planning and, for some, a reorganization of major industrial sectors, including the agriculture and energy industries. In contrast to apocalyptic environmentalism, so-called "emancipatory" environmentalism took a more positive and practical approach, one aspect of which was the effort to promote an ecological consciousness and an ethic of "stewardship" of the environment. One form of emancipatory environmentalism, human-welfare ecology—which aims to enhance human life by creating a safe and clean environment—was part of a broader concern with distributive justice and reflected the tendency, later characterized as "postmaterialist," of citizens in advanced industrial societies to place more importance on "quality-of-life" issues than on traditional economic concerns. Emancipatory environmentalism also was distinguished for some of its advocates by an emphasis on developing small-scale systems of economic production that would be more closely integrated with the natural processes of surrounding ecosystems. This more environmentally holistic approach to economic planning was promoted in work by the American ecologist Barry Commoner and by the German economist Ernst Friedrich Schumacher. In contrast to earlier thinkers who had downplayed the interconnectedness of natural systems, Commoner and Schumacher emphasized productive processes that worked with nature, not against it, encouraged the use of organic and renewable resources rather than synthetic products (e.g., plastics and chemical fertilizers), and advocated renewable and small-scale energy resources (e.g., wind and solar power) and government policies that supported effective public transportation and energy efficiency. The emancipatory approach was evoked through the 1990s in the popular slogan, "think globally, act locally." Its small-scale, decentralized planning and production has been criticized, however, as unrealistic in highly urbanized and industrialized societies.

BIOCENTRIC SCHOOLS OF THOUGHT

An emphasis on small-scale economic structures and the social dimensions of the ecological crisis also is a feature of the school of thought known as social ecology, whose major proponent was the American environmental anarchist Murray Bookchin. Social ecologists trace the causes of environmental degradation to the existence of unjust, hierarchical relationships in human society, which they see as endemic to the large-scale social structures of modern capitalist states. Accordingly, they argue, the most environmentally sympathetic form of political and social

Emancipatory environmentalism emphasized environmentally responsible economic planning, including the use of solar energy. Shutterstock.com

organization is one based on decentralized small-scale communities and systems of production.

A more radical doctrine, known as deep ecology, builds on preservationist themes from the early environmental movement. Its main originators, the Norwegian philosopher Arne Næss, the American sociologist Bill Devall, and the American philosopher George Sessions, share with social ecologists a distrust of capitalism and industrial technology and favour decentralized forms of social organization. Deep ecologists also claim that humans need to regain a "spiritual" relationship with nonhuman nature. By understanding the interconnectedness of all organisms—including humans—in the ecosphere and empathizing with nonhuman nature, they argue, humans would develop an ecological consciousness and a sense of ecological solidarity. The biocentric principle of interconnectedness was extensively developed by British environmentalist James Lovelock, who postulated in *Gaia: A New Look at Life on Earth* (1979) that the planet is a single living, self-regulating entity capable of reestablishing an ecological equilibrium, even without the existence of human life. Despite their emphasis on spirituality, some more extreme forms of deep ecology have been strongly criticized as antihumanist, on the ground that they entail opposition to famine relief and immigration and acceptance of large-scale losses of life caused by AIDS and other pandemics.

Oppression, hierarchy, and spiritual relationships with nature also have been central concerns of ecofeminism. Ecofeminists assert that there is a connection between the destruction of nature by humans and the oppression of women by men that arises from political theories and social practices in which both women and nature are treated as objects to be owned or controlled. Ecofeminists aim to establish a central role for women in the pursuit of an environmentally sound and socially just society. They have been divided, however, over how to conceive of the relationship between nature and women, which they hold is more intimate and more "spiritual" than the relationship between nature and men. Whereas cultural ecofeminists argue that the relationship is inherent in women's reproductive and nurturing roles, social ecofeminists, while acknowledging the relationship's immediacy, claim that it arises from social and cultural hierarchies that confine women primarily to the private sphere.

PACIFISM

Pacifism is the opposition to war and violence as a means of settling disputes. It may entail the belief that the waging

Norwegian philosopher Arne Næss was a key architect of deep ecology, a radical doctrine that develops preservationist ideas from the early environmental movement. Erlend Aas/AFP/Getty Images

of war by a state and the participation in war by an individual are absolutely wrong, under any circumstances.

EARLY RELIGIOUS AND PHILOSOPHICAL MOVEMENTS

In the ancient world, war was taken for granted as a necessary evil by some societies, while in others it was not even regarded as an evil. Individual voices in various lands decried the evils of war, but the first genuinely pacifist movement known came from Buddhism, whose founder demanded from his followers absolute abstention from any act of violence against their fellow creatures. In India the great Buddhist-influenced king Ashoka in the 3rd century BCE definitely renounced war, but he was thinking primarily of wars of conquest. In succeeding ages Buddhism does not seem to have been very successful in restraining the rulers of countries in which it was adopted from making war. This may be because the Buddhist rule of life, as generally understood, served as a counsel of perfection which comparatively few could be expected to follow in its entirety.

In classical antiquity, pacifism remained largely an ideal in the minds of a few intellectuals. The Greek conceptions of peace—including Stoicism—were centred on the peaceful conduct of the individual rather than on the conduct of whole peoples or kingdoms. In Rome the achievement of *pax,* or peace, was defined as a covenant between states or kingdoms that creates a "just" situation and that rests upon bilateral recognition. This judicial approach was applicable only to the "civilized world," however. Thus, the Pax Romana of the 1st and 2nd centuries CE was not really universal, because it was always regarded as a peace for the civilized world alone and excluded the barbarians. And since the barbarian threat never ended, neither did the wars Rome waged to protect its frontiers against this threat.

Christianity, with its evangelical message, offered considerations in support of individual nonviolence as well as of collective peacefulness. Jesus' spoken words as recorded in the New Testament could be interpreted as a kind of pacifism and in fact were so interpreted by many of Jesus' early radical followers. As a rule, however, the "peace" that Jesus spoke of was only open to minorities or to sects that practiced a rigorous ethics, while the Christian church itself had to compromise with worldly necessities. "The question of soldiers"—the inconsistency between the pursuit of peace and fighting in wars—was disturbing to Christians from the time of Jesus. However, in the early 3rd century, certain passages in the Gospels were interpreted to indicate that armies were not only acceptable but necessary in order to fight against demons. In the early 5th century, St. Augustine wrote *De civitate Dei* (*The City of God*), which presented a distinction between worldly and supraworldly peace. He felt that worldly peace was acceptable only if it was in accord with Christian law, and it was the duty of the worldly state to serve the church and to defend itself against those who wished to undermine the church's authority. These ideas prevailed throughout the Middle Ages and were often tied with the myth of an eschatological emperor who would suppress nonbelievers and lead the world to peaceful times. Like the Roman *pax,* Christian peace needed to be perpetually defended. There was a never-ending threat posed by non-Christians, who were viewed as demonic.

Political Influences

Since the Renaissance, concepts of pacifism have been developed with varying degrees of political influence. A great deal of pacifist thought in the 17th and 18th centuries was based on the idea that a transfer of political power from the sovereigns to the public was a crucial step toward world peace, since wars were thought of as arising from the dynastic ambitions and power politics of kings and princes. Thus was propagated the illusion that monarchies tended toward wars because the sovereigns regarded their states as their personal property and that compared to this, a republic would be peaceful. The offshoot of these theories was the creation of pacifist organizations in 19th-century Europe in which such ideas as general disarmament and the instigation of special courts to hear international conflicts were entertained. The theme of pacifism thereby caught the public interest and inspired an extensive literature. Some of these ideas were later realized in the Court of Arbitration in The Hague, the League of Nations, the United Nations, and temporary disarmament conferences, but their overall effect was limited. In the 19th century, for instance, the real maintenance of a relative peace resulted from the statesmanlike political establishment of a balance of power among the five great European states. The succeeding century, with its two world wars, its nuclear stalemate, and its unending succession of conflicts among developed and developing nations, has been notable chiefly for the utter irrelevance of pacifist principles and practices.

Pacifism is not a part of communist ideology. Lenin rejected it outright, and in the work of Karl Marx "revolution" and "war" are synonymous. Their theories and those of Friedrich Engels advocate the necessity of "just" war against the capitalistic classes, with the goals of a classless society and universal peace following the world-revolutionary victory of the international proletariat.

ARGUMENTS FOR AND AGAINST PACIFISM

There are two general approaches or varieties of pacifist behaviour and aspirations. The one rests on the advocacy of pacifism and the complete renunciation of war as a policy to be adopted by a nation. The other stems from the conviction of an individual that his personal conscience forbids him to participate in any act of war and perhaps in any act of violence whatsoever.

The arguments for pacifism as a possible national policy run on familiar lines. The obvious and admitted evils of war are stressed—the human suffering and loss of life, the economic damage, and, perhaps above all, the moral and spiritual degradation war brings. Since World War II increasing emphasis has also been laid on the terrible powers of destruction latent in nuclear weapons. Pacifist advocates often assume that the abandonment of war as an instrument of national policy will not be possible until the world community has become so organized that it can enforce justice among its members. The nonpacifist would, in general, accept what the pacifist says about the evils of war and the need for international organization. But he would claim that the pacifist has not faced squarely the possible evils that would result from the alternative policy of a nation's nonresistance in the face of external aggression: the possible mass deportations and even mass exterminations and the subjection of conquered peoples to totalitarian regimes that would suppress just those values which the pacifist stands for.

Pacifists may claim that these evils can be met by nonviolence (i.e., the principle and practice of abstaining from violence in all circumstances). Nonviolence could also mean nonviolent resistance, which relies on the difficulties and inconvenience that can be caused to the conqueror or oppressor by a general refusal of the public to cooperate. But recent history shows a striking number of occasions on which nonviolent tactics such as these entirely failed to disarm the enemy or even to preserve the communities practicing them. Pacifist Christian sects were often the objects of the most ruthless persecution in a time period stretching from the Middle Ages to the Nazi regime of Adolf Hitler. The story of the persecution of the Jews over many centuries is only too familiar, though for generations they practiced nonviolence toward their persecutors. It seems that pacifist or nonviolent methods can only be effective against a power that has no strong motives for going to extremes of suppression or one that is governed at least in part by the same moral scruples that actuate the pacifists themselves. It seems clear to most nonpacifists that complete nonresistance to external aggression would sooner or later lead to foreign domination of one's country, perhaps by the most fanatical and ruthless powers.

TYPES OF PACIFISM

Personal pacifism is a relatively common phenomenon compared with national pacifism. Members of several small Christian sects who try to literally follow the precepts of Jesus Christ have refused to participate in military service in many nations and have been willing to suffer the criminal or civil penalties that followed. Not all of these and other conscientious objectors are pacifists, but the great majority of conscientious objectors base their refusal to serve on their pacifist convictions. There are, moreover, wide differences of opinion among pacifists themselves about their attitude toward a community at war, ranging from the very small minority who would refuse to do anything that could help the national effort to those prepared to offer any kind of service short of actual fighting.

Conscientious Objector

A conscientious objector is one who opposes bearing arms or who objects to any type of military training and service. Some conscientious objectors refuse to submit to any of the procedures of compulsory conscription. Although all objectors take their position on the basis of conscience, they may have varying religious, philosophical, or political reasons for their beliefs.

Conscientious objection to military service has existed in some form since the beginning of the Common Era and has, for the most part, been associated with religious scruples against military activities. It developed as a doctrine of the Mennonites in various parts of Europe in the 16th century, of the Society of Friends in England in the 17th century, and of the Church of the Brethren and of the Dukhobors in Russia in the 18th century.

Throughout history, governments have been generally unsympathetic toward individual conscientious objectors; their refusal to undertake military service has been treated like any other breach of law. There have, however, been times when certain pacifistic religious sects have been exempted.

The relatively liberal policy of the United States began in colonial Pennsylvania, whose government was controlled until 1756 by Quaker pacifists.

Under the conscript laws of 1940, conscientious objector status, including some form of service unrelated to and not controlled by the military, was granted, but solely on the basis of membership in a recognized pacifistic religious sect.

In Great Britain a noncombatant corps was established during World War I, but many conscientious objectors refused to belong to it. During World War II, three types of exemption could be granted: (1) unconditional; (2) conditional on the undertaking of specified civil work; (3) exemption only from combatant duties. Conscription in Great Britain ended in 1960, and in 1968 recruits were allowed discharge as conscientious objectors within six months from the date of their entry into the military.

Scandinavian countries recognize all types of objectors and provide both noncombatant and civilian service. In Norway and Sweden civil defense is compulsory, with no legal recognition of objection to that type of service. A Swedish law of 1966 provided complete exemption from compulsory service for Jehovah's Witnesses. In the Netherlands, religious and moral objectors are recognized.

CONCLUSION

As this volume attests, the history of ethical theorizing in the West is both enormously varied and deeply continuous. Although the eudaemonism of Aristotle and the evolutionary ethics of E.O. Wilson are conceptually as well as temporally very remote, both identify what is morally good for human beings with the unimpeded operation of certain natural (or naturally selected) capacities. Epicurus's noble ethics of refined pleasure and friendship has distinct affinities with G.E. Moore's ideal utilitarianism, which aims at friendship and beauty as well as pleasure. The political liberalism of John Rawls is a far cry from that of John Locke (in fact, Locke's view is better described as libertarianism), but they are defended with strikingly similar conceptual constructs and methods of argument. In the area of metaethics, the sophisticated contemporary debates regarding the truth and objectivity of moral judgments can be dizzying in their technical sophistication, but they are essentially just elaborations of ancient positions. And while the practical problems addressed by contemporary applied ethics are in some cases completely new, almost all of the ethical perspectives from which they are examined would seem familiar to philosophers of the Enlightenment, if not also to those of ancient Greece.

In this respect the history of ethics is perhaps no different from most other branches of philosophy: progress is more often made by exploring and introducing variations on established themes than by replacing, lock, stock, and barrel, an old view with a new one. But Western ethics possesses another kind of continuity that may distinguish it among other philosophical endeavours, and that is the particular immediacy—indeed, urgency—of the questions it attempts to answer. The basic problems of ethics, in other words, seem to be a part of the "human condition": to be confronted with them is part of what it means to be a human being. And the ways in which we resolve, or at least struggle with, these problems helps to define the kind of human beings we are.

GLOSSARY

anarchism Political theory holding all forms of government authority to be unnecessary and undesirable and advocating a society based on voluntary cooperation and free association of individuals and groups.

bioethics Study of the philosophical, social, and legal issues arising in medicine and the life sciences; chiefly concerned with human life and well-being.

chauvinism Undue partiality or attachment to a group or place to which one belongs or has belonged.

compatibilism Thesis that free will, in the sense required for moral responsibility, is consistent with universal causal determinism.

conscientious objector One who opposes participation in military service, on the basis of religious, philosophical, or political belief.

corporeal Taking bodily form; tangible.

determinism In philosophy, the doctrine that all events, including human decisions, are completely determined by previously existing causes.

egoism In ethics, the principle that each person should act so as to promote his or her own interests.

Enlightenment European intellectual movement of the 17th and 18th centuries that emphasized the use of reason and science to combat injustice and oppression and to promote the material and moral progress of human society.

eudaemonism In ethics, the view that virtuous activity is a means toward and partly constitutive of human happiness, or flourishing.

euthanasia Act of painlessly killing or allowing to die persons with diseases, disorders, or injuries that will inevitably result in death.

feminism ,philosophical Loosely related set of approaches in various fields of philosophy that emphasizes the role of gender in the formation of traditional philosophical problems and concepts and the ways in which traditional philosophy reflects and perpetuates bias against women.

libertarianism Political philosophy that stresses personal liberty and that views governments with more than minimal powers as unjust.

logos (Greek: "word," "reason," "plan") In Greek philosophy and theology, the divine reason that orders the cosmos and gives it form and meaning.

metaethics Field of ethics concerned with ascertaining the nature of moral concepts and judgments primarily by examining the logical characteristics of moral concepts.

naturalism In metaethics, the view that moral values and judgments can be explained or assessed in terms of facts about the natural world.

pacifism The doctrine that war and violence as a means of settling disputes is morally wrong.

philosophes The philosophical, political, and social writers of 18th-century France.

polemical Aimed at attacking or refuting the views of another.

polis A city-state of ancient Greece.

postmaterialism Value orientation that accentuates self-expression and quality of life over economic and physical security.

speciesism Term used by some animal rights advocates to characterize the practice of favouring the interests of humans over the similar interests of other species.

stoicism Inspired by the teaching of Socrates and Diogenes of Sinope, Stoicism was founded at Athens

by Zeno of Citium c. 300 bce and was influential
throughout the Greco-Roman world until at least 200
ce. It stressed duty and held that, through reason,
humankind can come to regard the universe as governed by fate and, despite appearances, as
fundamentally rational. It maintained that, in regulat-
ing one's life, one can emulate the calm and order of
the universe by learning to accept events with a stern
and tranquil mind.

syllogism A deductive argument consisting of two categorical premises and a categorical conclusion.

teleological Concerning explanation by appeal to purpose, goal, design, or function.

totalitarianism Form of government that subordinates
all aspects of its citizens' lives to the authority of the
state, with a single charismatic leader as the ultimate
authority.

utilitarianism The doctrine that the moral rightness of
an action is determined by the amount or extent of
happiness it produces.

vegetarianism Theory or practice of abstaining from
eating flesh.

virtue ethics Approach to ethics that takes the notion
of virtue (often conceived as excellence) as
fundamental.

BIBLIOGRAPHY

EUDAEMONISM AND CONSEQUENTIALISM

Terence Irwin, *Plato's Ethics* (1995), is a broad treatment. Also of interest is Mary Margaret Mackenzie, *Plato on Punishment* (1981). Amélie Oksenberg Rorty (ed.), *Essays on Aristotle's "Ethics"* (1980, reissued 1996), is a valuable collection. Also of interest is Sarah Broadie, *Ethics with Aristotle* (1991).

Ludwig Edelstein, *The Meaning of Stoicism* (1966); and Josiah B. Gould, *The Philosophy of Chrysippus* (1970), are among the best of modern studies of Greco-Roman Stoicism.

A perceptive study of Epicurus's religiosity and ethics is Benjamin Farrington, *The Faith of Epicurus* (1967).

Secondary, historical, and contemporary studies of utilitarianism include David Lyons, *Forms and Limits of Utilitarianism* (1965); and Jan Narveson, *Morality and Utility* (1967).

CONTRACTUALISM AND DEONTOLOGY

A good general introduction to Hobbes is Tom Sorell, *Hobbes* (1986, reissued 1999). Useful studies of Locke include John Colman, *John Locke's Moral Philosophy* (1983); and Ruth W. Grant, *John Locke's Liberalism* (1987). Ronald Grimsley, *The Philosophy of Rousseau* (1973), provides a clear scholarly introduction to Rousseau's philosophical ideas.

Early critical responses to Rawls are collected in Norman Daniels (ed.), *Reading Rawls* (1974, reissued 1989).

Kant's critical ethics is discussed in Jeffrie G. Murphy, *Kant: The Philosophy of Right* (1970); and Viggo Rossvaer, *Kant's Moral Philosophy: An Interpretation of the Categorical Imperative* (1979).

Richard A. Epstein, *Simple Rules for a Complex World* (1995), argues for a system of law close to libertarianism on broadly utilitarian grounds.

FEMINISM AND EGOISM

Catharine A. MacKinnon, *Toward a Feminist Theory of the State* (1989), is the best presentation of her views. More mainstream perspectives are offered in Alison M. Jaggar, *Feminist Politics and Human Nature* (1983).

Egoism as a theory of rationality is discussed in David P. Gauthier (ed.), *Morality and Rational Self-Interest* (1970); and Ronald D. Milo (ed.), *Egoism and Altruism* (1973).

METAETHICS

Stephen Darwall, Allan Gibbard, and Peter Railton, *Moral Discourse and Practice: Some Philosophical Approaches* (1997), is an anthology that contains several important contributions to the modern debate over moral realism.

A philosophical defense of ethical relativism is Gilbert Harman, *Explaining Value and Other Esssays in Moral Philosophy* (2000). Thomas Nagel, *The Last Word* (1997), is a philosophical critique of relativism of all kinds, including ethical relativism.

Treatments of evolutionary ethics include Edward O. Wilson, *On Human Nature* (1978, reissued with a new preface, 2004); and Michael Bradie, *The Secret Chain: Evolution and Ethics* (1994).

APPLIED ETHICS

Helga Kuhse and Peter Singer (eds.), *A Companion to Bioethics* (1998), features reviews of key topics in the field.

Philosophical arguments for and against animal rights are explored in Andrew Linzey and P.B. Clarke (eds.), *Animal Rights: A Historic Anthology*, rev. ed. (2004). Cass R. Sunstein and Martha Craven Nussbaum (eds.), *Animal Rights: Current Debates and New Directions* (2004), is a collection of thought-provoking essays by philosophers, legal scholars, and scientists.

Michael E. Zimmerman (ed.), *Environmental Philosophy: From Animal Rights to Radical Ecology*, 3rd ed. (2001), includes discussion about key ideas in social ecology, deep ecology, and ecofeminism.

Michael Walzer, *Just and Unjust Wars: A Moral Argument with Historical Illustrations*, 3rd ed. (2000), is a fine study of the morality of war.

INDEX